CONTENTS

First published in the UK in 2019 by Studio Press Books,
an imprint of Bonnier Books UK
The Plaza, 535 King's Road, London, SW10 0SZ
www.studiopressbooks.co.uk
www.bonnierbooks.co.uk

© 2019 Studio Press

Written by Melanie Hamm

Cover illustration by Keith Robinson

A CIP catalogue record for this book is available from
the British Library.

Paperback: 978-1-78741-476-1

Printed and bound by Clays Ltd, Elcograf S.p.A

1 3 5 7 9 10 8 6 4 2

ULTIMATE SUPERSTARS

BEYONCÉ

For Andrew

CHAPTER 1

SUPER BOWL

Forgetting the words to a song had always been Beyoncé's greatest fear. It had been that way ever since she was a child, performing in talent shows in front of her parents and classmates. Of course, it hardly ever happened – and now, when it did, Bey was pretty good at styling it out.

But the worry still sprung up when she was nervous. And right now, she really was!

Beyoncé quickly pushed the thought away. When she was on tour, she performed to crowds as big as this almost every evening. She was one of the world's most famous entertainers. Standing in front of a crowd of seventy thousand people or more was normal to her!

But today more than 100 million viewers were also watching on TV.

The venue was the Levi's Stadium, Santa Clara, California. The event was Super Bowl 50, the fiftieth anniversary of the iconic American football championship final. The crowd had already watched an action-packed first half of football. The Denver Broncos were beating the Carolina Panthers 13–7. Coldplay had just rocked the stadium with a series of foot-stamping anthems. Now, Bruno Mars and Mark Ronson were onstage, delivering an effortlessly cool performance of their new song, 'Uptown Funk'.

As the song reached its energetic finale, six flares shot up into the sky. The smoke trailed away, then, down on the pitch, a wall of fireworks sizzled into life. This was the drummers' cue to hit their beat.

Boom. Boom. Boom.

Bey waited between the rows of drummers, still hidden from the crowd. She began the countdown in her head, in time with the beat of the drums. *Boom. Boom. Boom. Ten. Nine. Eight.*

The beat got louder and louder. *Seven. Six. Five.*

The drummers began to peel away, to the left and to the right. *Four. Three. Two.*

One. Suddenly Beyoncé was alone, striding up the pitch to the beat of the drums, wearing her trademark bodysuit, her hair billowing behind her like a flame.

Her first notes were soft. Three lines of dancers began to move, one behind Beyoncé, one either side of her, moving together in perfect time. Bey's voice swelled with each line of song. Then, at last, she unleashed its full power. As she did so, columns of yellow flames soared up into the air. The crowd greeted her new song, 'Formation', with wild delight.

Moments later, Bey and her dancers strode off the pitch and onto the stage, facing Bruno Mars and his dancers in a dance-off. The opening notes of 'Crazy in Love' rang through the stadium. This was the song everyone knew – one of Bey's biggest hits.

'Crazy in Love' trailed into 'Uptown Funk' as Beyoncé and Bruno Mars were joined by Coldplay's Chris Martin. Suddenly, the three megastars were singing together. The audience's cheers were at fever pitch.

Then the crowd's attention was directed to the big screen. A video montage showed the most iconic singers who had performed in fifty years of Super Bowl half-time shows: Michael Jackson, Stevie Wonder, Madonna, Bruce Springsteen, Diana Ross, James Brown, Prince and... Beyoncé herself, only four years earlier. Yes, Bey had achieved what just a handful of singers had – she had performed at the Super Bowl twice!

Even for a singer as famous as Bey, it was an amazing feeling to watch herself on the giant screen alongside so many legendary artists. Some of them she had admired since she was a child. These were the greatest singers in the world.

And she had earned her place among them.

Life didn't get much bigger or better than this.

CHAPTER 2

WHAT'S IN A NAME?

"When she grows up, she's going to be so mad at you!"

Lumis Beyincé cradled his tiny granddaughter in his arms. There was a broad smile on his face. The baby he held was perfect: beautiful, healthy *and* sleeping peacefully. But her name – surely it must be a joke?

"Beyoncé? You can't call her that! It's not a name!"

"It is now," said Tina, Lumis's daughter, firmly.

"Beyoncé." Lumis tried it out again. "Beyoncé. Just wait till she gets to school. She'll be picked on. You'll see."

"I don't want our family name to die out, Dad,"

explained Tina. When she married, Tina had taken her husband's surname: Knowles. "She's Beyoncé. Like Beyincé, our name. It's unique, just like her." She gazed proudly at her sleeping child.

Lumis frowned. "What does Mathew think?"

"Mathew has chosen her middle name. *And* she'll have his surname," Tina reminded him. "This way she has names from both of us."

Lumis was far from convinced. "Well, it's memorable," he said. "I suppose that's something."

Beyoncé Giselle Knowles had been born just a few days earlier, on 4 September 1981, in Park Plaza Hospital, Houston. Her parents, Tina and Mathew, thought she was the most beautiful baby they had ever seen. She had long, thick eyelashes, big, soulful eyes and plenty of dark curly hair. Mathew was so proud of his new daughter that he took her everywhere with him, showing her off to his friends and even his work colleagues.

"She's special, this one," he said to Tina. "She's got her mother's beauty *and* her voice, too. This is a girl you can't ignore..."

Tina laughed. The piercing howls of a newborn certainly took some getting used to. And when baby Beyoncé cried, she *really* cried.

"She's a good girl," said Tina. "But I wish she wasn't *quite* so loud!"

Baby Beyoncé's parents had married in January of the previous year. Mathew was a salesperson, working for Xerox. Tina had just finished training as a hairdresser and beautician. She was delighted at the arrival of baby Bey – but, she had to admit, it was bad timing. Up till now, she had been using a room in their house as a salon. But word had got around: Tina was good! She needed more space, in order to accommodate a growing list of clients. She needed a proper salon, with staff.

So Tina had bought a small salon and furnished it. She was excited – this was the start of the career she had dreamed of. Her job allowed her to be both independent and creative. She loved her work.

But she also had a baby!

"I want to go back to the salon, Mathew," she told her husband, soon after Bey was born. "I want my daughter to understand the importance of being independent."

Mathew understood. He was just as ambitious as Tina. When he was a teenager, he had won a scholarship to the University of Tennessee at Chattanooga. He had been one of first African-Americans to attend the university. Later, he had excelled as a salesperson and won promotion after promotion. When he decided to do something, Mathew gave it his all.

"Let's ask my mother – I'm sure she'll be able to help," he said. "She adores Beyoncé."

Mathew was right. His mother, Lue Helen, did agree to help. So while baby Beyoncé was looked after by her grandmother, Tina worked hard to make a success of her new salon, Headliners. She was proud of the name. Of course, she had to choose a pun – what hair salon didn't have a pun? Hairway to Heaven, Millionhairs... the list was endless. Tina also wanted to make the women she styled feel as glamorous as actresses, singers and models. Why couldn't they be the star of their own show, the headline act?

While Tina's salon began to thrive, little Beyoncé was growing, too. Before her parents knew it, she was crawling – then walking. As soon as she was able to toddle around on her tiny legs, Bey was dancing – or something that resembled it! Whenever music came on the radio, Bey wobbled and swayed in time to the beat. Every time Tina and Mathew played one of their records, she clapped her small hands with delight. If they tried to pick her up while the music was playing, she would wriggle away. She liked cuddles, but she loved dancing more!

And soon, little Bey was babbling away to the melody, too. She couldn't say many words yet, but that didn't stop her from joining in. While the grown-ups chatted, she gabbled to herself, happy in her own little world.

By the time she was three, Beyoncé was able to sing along to her favourite tunes. Whenever Tina and Mathew were too busy to play with her, they knew Bey would be content on her own, singing along to a record or watching a talent show on TV.

By the time she was five, Bey's favourite

singer was Michael Jackson. She watched his performances, captivated...

She learned every note of every song – and every step of his dance routines. She performed them so often that eventually Mathew and Tina knew them by heart, too!

"We should take her to a concert," Mathew suggested one day.

"She's only five!" Tina laughed. "Surely she's too young for a pop concert?"

"But she loves music," said Mathew.

The next day, Mathew came home with tickets to a Michael Jackson show. Beyoncé shrieked for joy. This was the most exciting thing she could imagine in the world! She flung her arms around her dad's waist and he lifted her into the air.

"Now you can sing along to the real thing!" he told her.

CHAPTER 3

MICHAEL JACKSON

Time seemed to stand still as Bey waited for the day of the concert to come round. She felt so impatient! Why did she have to go to school? Why did she have to go to the mall with her mom? Why did she have to help her dad wash the car? Nothing – apart from watching her Michael Jackson videos – made the time pass any quicker. She wished someone could wave a magic wand and transport her straight to the day of the show.

Eventually, the big day came.

"You still have to go to school, honey," Tina told her daughter.

"I can't. I feel sick, Mommy."

"You're excited, that's all. The day will go so

quickly, you won't even notice it."

And somehow it did. Tina dropped her off at school. Beyoncé took her seat in class. She did her lessons and ate her lunch in the cafeteria. But inside, Bey wasn't really there. She was already at the concert, staring at the dazzling lights on the stage, waiting for her hero to appear...

At long last, Tina arrived to pick her up. Bey jumped into the car like an action hero. "Quick, Mommy, drive!"

"But there's no rush, sweetie. The concert doesn't start for hours."

Beyoncé flung herself back against the leather of the seat, her face scrunched into a grimace. It still wasn't time? Impossible! Her whole body was tingling. "I'm going to explode, Mommy. I can feel it!"

Tina laughed. "Hang on in there, honey," she joked. "Your dad and me, we'd be so upset if you exploded. It would be such bad timing... Who on earth could we ask to take your ticket at such short notice?"

Bey smiled. Her mum always made things

better. But still... she didn't know how she would survive until the evening!

Once dinner was eaten and Bey had picked an outfit, finally – finally! – it was time to leave. Mathew drove them through Houston, towards the stadium. Bey felt so grown-up – she was on her way to a concert with her parents. How stylish her mum and dad looked! Bey hoped she would be as glamorous as her mum when she was older.

There weren't many kids in the audience – at least, not many as young as Bey. The crowd was mostly teens and grown-ups. Bey sat between her parents. They had brought cushions for her to sit on, so she would be able to see above the heads of the people in front. Bey gazed around the stadium with wide eyes. She had never seen so many people in her life; there were thousands and thousands of fans, all cheering and whooping, waiting for their hero.

"He won't sing straight away," Mathew explained. "First, there will be a warm-up act."

Bey nodded. She knew about opening acts. And

although there were butterflies in her stomach, now that she was here in the stadium, she didn't mind waiting. At last she knew it was real, and not a dream that might suddenly disappear!

In fact, Bey enjoyed the opening act. She didn't know the songs, but new music always interested her. Her heart leapt every time a song finished and the audience burst into applause. Bey joined them, clapping enthusiastically. It was amazing to be part of this huge crowd, reacting as one.

And then it was time...

The stage lights dimmed. Bey clutched her parents' hands. The audience had grown silent, but somehow the silence was louder than the cheers and applause. It was full of expectation, as if everyone in the crowd were holding their breath.

Suddenly Bey felt that tingling again, like she might explode at any second. Tina squeezed her hand.

"Breathe, honey!" she whispered.

Out of the darkness came a flash of lightning and a rumble of thunder. A snare drum rattled, the howl of a werewolf... followed by the opening notes of 'Thriller'. But still Bey couldn't take a breath. Not yet. Not until...

There he was!

A slim figure wearing a red sequinned jacket. Michael Jackson... MJ!

He flung his arms wide, as if embracing the audience. The crowd erupted into wild cheers of delight and Bey felt an explosion of joy inside her. It was as if her heart had leapt out of her chest and was soaring above the stadium. When Mathew and Tina looked at their little daughter, her eyes were shining, her gaze locked upon the stage. Nothing could have prised her from her seat.

Bey was transfixed. She didn't take her eyes from her hero as he performed 'Thriller'. When the song ended, and the eruption of cheers and applause came, she couldn't join in. She was still inside the song. Without thinking, she held her breath again till the notes of the next song began.

One after another, MJ's songs rocked the stadium: 'Don't Stop 'Til You Get Enough', 'Billie Jean', 'Bad', 'The Man in the Mirror'...

But the biggest cheers were reserved for MJ's

signature dance move: the moonwalk. The singer was wearing sequinned socks that sparkled with every step. Bey had seen these moves many times on video, but seeing MJ perform them live, they seemed so much faster. How did he do it? She couldn't believe a real person could dance like that. It was like magic.

And watching her hero, Beyoncé knew that one day she wanted to do this, too. She wanted to perform in front of an audience and make them think that magic was happening.

CHAPTER 4

IMAGINE

A year had passed since the Michael Jackson concert. Beyoncé was now six. Listening to music was still the thing that made Bey happiest. She loved to sing and make up dance moves.

But Tina was worried.

"She doesn't have any friends," she said to Mathew. "Why isn't she outside, playing with the other kids?"

At school, Beyoncé was quiet. She was so scared of speaking in front of the other kids that she never put her hand up in class. At lunch and break times, she played by herself. She didn't get invited to parties and sleepovers like the other children.

"She's shy," said Mathew.

"I think she's being bullied," said Tina.

Tina was right. Most of the other children were loud and outgoing. They didn't understand shy, nervous Beyoncé. They thought she was unfriendly and stuck-up because she didn't talk to them. She also looked different. Bey was lighter-skinned than the other children. Tina was Creole, and Bey had inherited her mum's caramel-coloured skin. Having an unusual name didn't help, either. Beyoncé? What kind of a name was that?!

Yes, Bey was different, and the other children didn't let her forget it.

"I want her to be happy," sighed Tina. "I wish I knew how to help."

Tina was used to her little daughter not telling her much about school. She knew Bey didn't enjoy it much, so she didn't press her for details. But one day, Beyoncé surprised her.

"Teacher taught us a song today," she told her mum when they arrived home.

"Let's hear it then," said Tina, smiling. She loved to hear her daughter sing. Bey had a pretty, tuneful voice. But all parents thought their children were special, didn't they?

Tina did not expect this...

Bey took a deep breath. She opened her mouth wide and suddenly her sweet, clear voice filled the room. It was only a children's song; the words and the tune were simple. But, somehow, Bey made it sound extraordinary. She sang with a confidence Tina had never seen or heard in her before. Beyoncé stood tall and tilted her head proudly, holding her mother's gaze from the first note to the last, as if she were a singer onstage.

After the last notes trickled away, Tina asked, "Did Teacher show you how to sing it like that?"

"No, I made it up."

Tina shook her head in disbelief. While she was singing, shy, quiet Bey had come alive. Her eyes had shone. Her face had lit up. Her whole body had moved to the rhythm of the song. It was as if her daughter had been transformed.

Tina knew she had witnessed something magical.

It wasn't long before Beyoncé's teachers at school

saw it, too. Lots of young kids were good singers, but Beyoncé Knowles had real talent. While the other children took weeks to learn a tune and hit the right notes, Bey grasped new songs instantly. Then she began to make them her own: varying the rhythm, adding harmonies and little musical flourishes.

Every time she performed in front of her teachers and classmates, Bey grew in confidence. Her teachers could see how much she loved to be onstage. Like Tina, they were happy to see shy Beyoncé come out of her shell for a few minutes while she sang.

Bey was seven when a talent show between local schools was announced. Her teachers decided to enter her. Most of the competitors would be teenagers, but Beyoncé was so advanced that they knew the judges would be impressed.

After school, Bey's music teacher told Tina of the plan. Together, the teachers had even chosen a song: 'Imagine' by John Lennon.

"It suits her voice," said Bey's teacher, smiling down at her.

"But she's so young," said Tina. "Are you sure about this?"

"I want to, Mommy," said Bey, tugging on her mother's skirt.

It wasn't hard to persuade Tina to let Bey take part in the competition. Onstage, Bey performed with such skill and confidence.

"You'll be competing against much older children," Tina warned her daughter. "Just do your best. I'll always be proud of you."

But Beyoncé shook her head. "I'm going to *win*, Mommy."

The evening of the talent show quickly came round. With the help of her teachers, Bey had practised hard. She could feel excitement and nerves bubbling up inside her, but she did her best to stay calm. She ate her dinner: gumbo, a Creole dish, her favourite. She put on the dress that Tina had laid out for her, and her best shoes. Bey usually preferred shorts and T-shirts, but singers had to look special onstage, she knew that. Her hero, Michael Jackson, always did! Then she sat quietly while Tina combed her curly hair into bunches and tied brightly coloured ribbons around them.

"You're very quiet, honey," said Tina. "Are you nervous?"

"I'm *focusing*, Mommy," said Beyoncé. "That's what singers do."

Tina smiled. Her little Bey was going to be just fine.

In the school hall, there were so many rows of seats that Bey couldn't count them. Tina, Mathew and Beyoncé's new baby sister, Solange, found a place near the front. Proud parents were still hurrying into the hall. Everyone wanted to sit near the stage. No one wanted to miss a thing.

Then the show began.

Backstage, Bey listened to each act in turn. Some of the kids were singing alone; some as duos or groups. Some played instruments, too. Most were singing classic songs, like she was, but a few had written music of their own.

Bey might only be seven, but she could pick out the good singers easily.

Oh, she's amazing!

No – that's not in the right key.

He went wrong at the end.

She's good, but she needs to work on the high notes.

And, because it was a talent show, it wasn't only singers who were performing. There were rappers, dancers, even a boy performing magic. It was hard to tell which performances the audience liked best – every act received enthusiastic applause.

It was almost time for Bey to go onstage. Only one act to go! Bey had been so calm, but as she waited in the wings, suddenly she was shaking with fear. All those seats... All those people!

Then she heard: *"Please put your hands together to welcome seven-year-old Beyoncé Knowles, singing 'Imagine'..."*

Beyoncé's teacher reached for her hand and gently propelled her onto the stage.

Bey could hear her dad's booming applause from where she stood in the spotlight. Both of her parents were smiling straight at her. In an instant, her nerves melted away.

And when Bey smiled, it was for the whole

audience. Every single person needed to know she was singing for them...

When the song ended, Bey felt like she was returning to earth. She wasn't sure where she had travelled to, but it was very far away – beyond the school hall, beyond Houston, up into the clouds somewhere. Beyoncé had felt like a different person when the spotlight was on her and she was performing.

She heard the audience cheering. How loud they were! Had the applause been this loud before, when the other acts sang?

And then she saw they were on their feet. A standing ovation!

The applause rang in Bey's ears as she ran offstage. She hadn't been nervous while she was singing – but she was now. Would she win? Or would the audience love the next act even more? She really hoped they wouldn't. She wanted to win so badly!

Once again, little Beyoncé forced herself to be calm. And wait.

CHAPTER 5

HOME

"And the winner is... Beyoncé Knowles!"

Bey hardly dared believe it! Suddenly, she was back onstage. At least the audience thought she was. In Bey's head, she was up in the clouds again, in her own little world.

"Congratulations, Beyoncé! You have an amazing voice for such a young singer. Are your mom and dad here tonight?" asked the host.

Beyoncé dragged herself back down to earth. What was the question? Her parents?

"Er, yes, they're over there." She pointed at Mathew, Tina and little Solange, who was sitting on Papa's knee, playing with her toy.

Mathew waved back, causing Solange to drop

her toy and let out a squeal of dismay. The people around them laughed.

The compère handed Bey the trophy. "I think this will be the first of many prizes, Beyoncé Knowles! Let's have one more round of applause for our young winner..."

Bey held on tightly to the little statuette. *The first of many? Wow!* All she knew was that this was where she wanted to be for ever – onstage, with an audience cheering her!

Seeing how happy Bey was while she was performing, Tina had an idea. What if Bey were to enter some local pageants? There were lots of children's pageants in Houston. They were partly beauty contests – the girls had to dress up in pretty dresses – and partly talent competitions. Tina knew her daughter didn't really care about dressing up like a princess, but she also knew Bey would love the talent-show element. She would start entering Bey into some local competitions. It would bring her out of her shell, Tina was sure. It would help her to make friends.

So, most weekends, Tina and Mathew took Beyoncé to a pageant. Little Solange came, too – and sometimes begged to be allowed to take part with her big sister.

Tina's mother, Agnèz, had been a dressmaker. She had made all of Tina's dresses when she was a girl: elaborate dresses in beautiful colours, covered in frills and ribbons. Tina had inherited her skill, and she made Beyoncé a beautiful outfit for each competition, each dress fancier than the last.

Tina was right. Beyoncé wasn't interested in the sparkling dresses, but she loved to be up onstage. She loved rehearsing her performances at home. She was never bored when she had a new song to learn. She practised it over and over again until every word, every note and every gesture was perfect.

Soon, Beyoncé's bedroom was full of trophies. She won every show that her parents entered her into. Her lovely voice, her charm and grace never failed to win the judges' votes. Eventually, there were 30 awards, of every shape and size, carefully arranged on her shelf.

There was only one problem...

Onstage, Bey brimmed with confidence, but offstage she was still as shy as ever. She hadn't made friends as Tina had hoped. *It's like she is two completely different people,* her mother thought anxiously.

Tina was puzzled – and she continued to worry about her quiet little girl. Bey loved taking care of her sister, Solange, but Solange wasn't even at school yet. She wasn't old enough to be a proper friend to her sister. Tina wanted Bey to have fun. She wanted Bey to have friends her own age to play with.

Would it ever happen?

When Beyoncé was eight, Tina and Mathew entered her into the children's category of the prestigious Sammy Awards. It was the biggest talent show Bey had taken part in so far, and she was excited. She had a new song to sing: 'Home', from the film *The Wiz*. The film was based on the story *The Wizard of Oz*, and Beyoncé had watched it over and over again. The singer Diana Ross played Dorothy, who meets a friendly scarecrow, a tin man and a lion on her adventures in the Land of Oz. Beyoncé was spellbound every time she listened to Diana's beautiful voice. She wanted to sing just like that!

There would be a very large audience for the awards. Tina made Bey a special costume: a blue pinafore covered in sequins, and a white blouse. Bey wore them with white tights and red shoes.

"You look just like Dorothy," she said proudly, kissing her daughter. "Doesn't she, Solange?"

"Bey... Dorotee," lisped little Solange.

Bey had been practising her song for weeks, but she was still nervous. She was always nervous – right up till the moment she stepped onto the stage. There, something magical happened and her nerves would flutter away.

"Just do your best," Mathew said, giving her a hug. "The rest is up to the audience."

The community centre where the competition was taking place was full to bursting. From their seats in the middle of the hall, Mathew and Tina waited eagerly to see their daughter. Solange spotted the host and began to clap her tiny hands with excitement.

"Bey! Bey! Bey!" she cried. She loved to see her big sister perform.

A few rows in front of them, two other audience members were watching the stage keenly.

Denise Seals and Deborah Laday had a special reason for being at the competition. As the host introduced the first act, all of their attention was focused on the singer. The girl, aged about ten, was nervous. She had a nice voice, but it trembled when she reached the high notes. Denise and Deborah shook their heads. *Not what we're looking for.*

The next act came on. It was three young boys, singing and rapping. They bounded energetically across the stage. The audience loved them. But – *Not right, either.*

Several more acts performed. Deborah sighed. These children were good, but...

"Are we ever going to find what we're looking for?" she whispered to Denise. "We must have watched two hundred children sing by now."

The crowd hushed once more. A girl in a sparkly blue pinafore dress and red shoes stepped onto the stage. The host introduced her and held out the microphone. The girl took it calmly. She smiled. There was silence for a couple of seconds as she gazed out at her audience, then she began to sing.

CHAPTER 6

GIRL'S TYME

Denise and Deborah couldn't take their eyes off the stage. They didn't say a word, but as the girl in the blue pinafore sang, each knew what the other was thinking: *she's perfect*.

They barely listened while the rest of the acts performed. There was a pause while the judges made their decision, but Denise and Deborah already knew who the winner would be – the little girl who had sung 'Home'; Beyoncé Knowles.

It was easy to spot Beyoncé's parents after the show had finished. They had the biggest smiles of anyone, and little Solange was still shouting "Bey! Bey!" from her father's arms. Then Beyoncé herself came running up to them and the whole family hugged.

"Well done, honey! That was brilliant!"

While groups of people congratulated Beyoncé, Denise and Deborah took her parents aside to speak to them. How proud they must be! Did they expect their daughter to win?

"Of course!" said Mathew.

Tina nodded, smiling.

Then Denise and Deborah explained why they had come to the competition. They were looking for talented girls to join their R&B singing group.

"It's called Girl's Tyme," said Denise.

"Because it's time girls were centre stage," explained Deborah. "We want everyone to see just how much talent our young girls have."

"That's true," Tina and Mathew agreed.

Denise smiled down at Beyoncé. "Would you be interested in auditioning for the group?" she asked.

Bey nodded shyly.

"Me too!" cried Solange, who was never shy.

"You're a bit too young," laughed Mathew. "Your time will come, Solange."

"Beyoncé would love to audition, though," said Tina. "Thank you."

The following week, Beyoncé sang again for Denise and Deborah. They already knew how great her voice was, but would she sound good with the other girls? They wanted to find three girls whose voices complemented each other. They wanted a group with star quality.

Eventually, they picked three girls: Beyoncé, Staci LaToisen and Jennifer Young. Staci was ten; Jennifer, eleven. Aged eight, Bey was the youngest of the group.

"Welcome to Girl's Tyme!" Denise told them.

"You all want to be singers? We want to help you," said Deborah.

The three girls looked at each other and smiled shyly. They all dreamed of becoming stars, and they knew this was an amazing chance!

Deborah and Denise also managed two other groups. Deborah's daughter, Millicent, whose stage name was M-1, was a rapper. The second group was a hip-hop dance duo called Destiny, made up of two girls called LaTavia Roberson and Chris Lewis, both aged nine. Denise and Deborah were planning a show featuring all three acts.

"We'll give you vocal training," Deborah told them. "Then we'll organise shows for you to perform in, all over Houston. We'll invite record-label scouts to watch you."

It was the most exciting thing that had ever happened to Beyoncé. She would get to do even more of what she loved most: singing. And now she had other girls to do it with!

Tina was delighted. Finally, shy Beyoncé had found a group of girls who she seemed comfortable with. These girls could be just the friends her daughter needed.

The singing training started immediately. Most evenings, the girls' parents dropped them off at Denise and Deborah's office. Denise was in charge of coaching the girls. She showed them techniques for strengthening their voices. They practised harmonies. She taught them how to give each song more expression.

All the girls found their voices getting stronger and more powerful as the weeks went by. But no one asked as many questions as Beyoncé!

She wanted to know every detail. How could she produce different types of sound? Which techniques were useful for hitting the high notes? Why did some notes sound good together, while other notes sounded awful?

She also knew the particular strengths of the other girls.

"Staci should sing that part. And that one would be best for Jennifer. Her voice is the lowest. If we sing it like this, we'll get a good harmony."

Denise laughed. She had never met a young girl who picked everything up so quickly.

"She's extraordinary," she told Deborah. "You'd think she was ten years older."

Girl's Tyme were practising hard and it wasn't long before Denise decided that they needed an audience. Tina had the perfect idea: the girls could sing at Headliners. There was a captive audience, after all.

So they did, several times a week. Tina's customers loved to be entertained – mostly!

"Didn't we hear that song last week, Beyoncé?"

said a regular client. "You girls need more songs if you're going to sing here as much as you do!"

"I don't like that last one," another client grumbled. "It's too modern. Why don't you sing us a classic?"

Bey and her new friends loved hanging out at the salon. It was much bigger than it used to be. Tina had even started giving makeovers, in addition to doing hair. Bey liked to watch as her mum studied her client's face, then picked out eyeshadows and lipsticks. Her mum's make-up box was like a treasure chest, filled with glittering colours of every shade, and tins and tubes of sweet-smelling gels and creams. Next, Tina would take brushes and, in front of Bey's eyes, the client would be transformed. It was like magic. Or getting dressed up for a show.

Most of all, though, Bey loved listening to the women in the salon as they swapped stories. They trusted each other with their secrets, their joys and sorrows. They helped each other, with advice and hugs. Sometimes they just listened and that was enough. Bey was a shy and serious child. She was interested in what her mother and her clients had to say about life – the big things and the small things. She felt at home at Headliners.

Performing at the salon was great practice for the girls, but Deborah and Denise knew Girl's Tyme was ready for a real stage. The first concert was booked for Hobart Taylor Hall at Prairie View A&M University. Girl's Tyme and the other acts, M-1 and Destiny, would be appearing as part of a youth showcase. There would be two thousand people in the audience.

"Two thousand people!" whispered Beyoncé nervously. How would she spot Tina, Mathew and Solange in a crowd of two thousand faces?

But being part of a group was brilliant. Before, when Bey had been scared, there was no one to share her fear with. Now, she had five friends who were just as nervous as she was. It made her feel so much better.

CHAPTER 7

GETTING SERIOUS

"Ladies and gentlemen, you are about to experience the ultimate masterpiece – M-1, Destiny and Girl's Tyme..."

As the crowd burst into applause, Bey's heart leapt. She was about to go onstage as part of a group for the very first time! She squeezed Staci and Jennifer's hands as they ran on together. She wasn't sure they were performing a masterpiece, but it felt amazing anyway.

Backstage, Denise and Deborah beamed with pride. They had watched for weeks and months as the girls' performances got stronger and more polished. And it wasn't only their singing. In addition to vocal coaching, Denise and Deborah had hired a choreographer to teach dance routines to the girls. Keith Bell was a young dancer and he was full of ideas. The girls had ideas of their own, too: they wanted to dance like their favourite R&B artists and pop stars!

"Those girls can really move," Deborah said proudly.

"They own the stage," smiled Denise.

The audience agreed. Two thousand people gave Bey and her friends a standing ovation. Their first showcase was a triumph.

Denise and Deborah were working hard at booking new concerts for the girls. That wasn't all, though. There were also auditions for music showcases and even TV commercials. A company called Pro-Line chose LaTavia to star in adverts for their hair products. All the girls were jealous – except Beyoncé, who was really only interested in singing!

Now, Bey and her friends were rehearsing every single night. Bey would come straight home from school to start her homework. Then she would go to the rehearsal studio at 6 p.m. for vocal training with Denise and dance practice with Keith.

In between songs, the girls would finish their homework. Finally, at 9 p.m., they could go home. It was lots of fun – but very tiring!

Denise and Deborah were delighted with how things were going. Audiences loved their show. The girls were happy and getting more and more confident. But there was a problem – and it wouldn't go away.

"We need more money," Deborah said to Denise anxiously.

It was only a few months since they had started their talent management company. So far, they were spending more money than they were making.

"We have new bills for the office and rehearsal studio." Deborah sighed.

"And for hiring concert venues," added Denise.

Denise and Deborah also had to buy costumes for the girls and pay for the music they performed. Most importantly, if they wanted to get a record deal for the girls, they would need to pay for sessions in a recording studio. Record labels would only consider recordings of professional quality.

"We need an investor," said Deborah. "Someone

who believes in the girls and their future as much as we do."

"Those girls are brilliant!" said Denise. "We'll find someone."

She felt sure that the right person would turn up soon.

Denise was right. Within a few weeks, she and Deborah were contacted by just the investor they needed. Her name was Andretta Tillman, and she fell in love with Girl's Tyme the moment she saw them. "They're amazing singers," she declared. "They have real stage presence."

Andretta had always been interested in music. She was a widow, and when her husband was alive, they had dreamed of setting up a record label for young artists. Girl's Tyme were so talented! Perhaps this was Andretta's opportunity to make that dream come true...

"I'll give you the money," she told Denise and Deborah. "But I want to co-manage the girls with you. I want to make some changes."

"We're listening," said Denise and Deborah.

"I want to hire a producer and songwriter," Andretta told them. "His name is Lonnie Jackson. He'll help make the girls into stars."

Denise and Deborah were nervous of change, but they wanted the best for the girls. They believed Beyoncé and her friends were capable of amazing things. So they agreed to Andretta's suggestion.

"Lonnie might want to do things differently," Andretta warned them.

Denise and Deborah nodded. "We'll do whatever it takes."

Nine-year-old Bey didn't really understand what was going on behind the scenes with Girl's Tyme. All she knew was that there were now more people working hard to make the group a success. Including a producer. Surely that was a good thing! She was excited to sing for Lonnie and Andretta – to show them what she could do.

The girls performed their show for Lonnie, Andretta and their parents one evening after school. As usual, Millicent bounded onto the stage first, rapping as M-1. Then Destiny did their dance routine. Finally, Girl's Tyme closed the show with a dazzling finale, performing the songs Bey, Staci and Jennifer had all worked so hard on.

Everyone applauded loudly.

"Well done, girls," said Andretta. "Great performances."

"Take a break, girls," Deborah told them. "It's time to do some homework."

When the girls had left the room, Lonnie delivered his news. "There are too many girls," he said.

"You want boys, too?" asked Denise. "But our idea was to promote female talent."

"No – I mean, there are too many different acts. We need to focus on a few of them."

"I agree," said Andretta. "If we want to succeed, the group needs to be recognisable. Just three or four singers."

The parents stared at Andretta and Lonnie in dismay. Deborah and Denise gulped. They loved all the girls. They hated the idea of losing a single one of them.

"Who do you want to keep?" they asked nervously.

"First, LaTavia," said Lonnie...

Andretta nodded. "She's got such a big personality."

"And Beyoncé. That's it."

Deborah and Denise look at each other. "But that's only two girls. You said three or four."

"We'll audition for two more."

So Staci, Jennifer, Millicent and Chris would be leaving the group... Denise exchanged glances with the parents. Everyone felt sick at the thought of telling the girls. They had all worked so hard.

Deborah put her head in her hands. She knew how upset her daughter, Millicent, would be.

"But I understand," she added generously. "And I believe every one of these girls will succeed on her own."

Denise nodded. "They all have such talent."

"Lonnie's going to write the music for the group," continued Andretta. "And the lyrics will be written by Anthony Moore. You'll meet him soon."

"I'm sorry. I know the girls will be very disappointed," said Lonnie. He looked round at the parents whose daughters would be leaving the group. "I hope *all* the girls will go on to be stars."

Tina and Mathew glanced at each other. Thank goodness! Bey would have been devastated to leave Girl's Tyme. They knew how talented their daughter was. They were so relieved that Lonnie and Andretta could see it, too.

Auditions for two new singers took place the following week. Lonnie and Andretta, Denise and Deborah listened to hundreds of girls. They had come with their families from all over Houston, and farther, excited at the idea of joining an all-girl group.

There were two girls who stood out.

Kelendria Rowland was ten. She had a wonderfully clear and powerful voice.

"Like a young Whitney Houston," said Lonnie admiringly.

But Kelendria was very shy. Would she be too nervous to stand onstage in front of crowds of people?

"Bey is shy, too," Denise told Lonnie. "That has never stopped her."

"Those two will get along well," added Deborah.

Kelendria – or Kelly – was in.

The second girl was called Ashley Davis. She was eleven, but when she sang, she sounded like she was at least eighteen. Her voice was full and rich – more mature even than Beyoncé's.

"She's got an amazing range," said Andretta. "She's perfect for Girl's Tyme."

It was decided. Kelly and Ashley would both join the group. Ashley would sing lead vocals with Beyoncé. Kelly would be a backing singer. LaTavia would rap. Andretta and Lonnie also found two new dancers: LaTavia's cousins, Nicki and Nina Taylor.

The line-up was complete.

CHAPTER 8

BEST FRIENDS

It was sad not to be hanging out with Staci, Jennifer and the others who had left the group – but Bey quickly got used to spending time with the new girls. They got on instantly; it was like having five new sisters. Bey and Kelly were best friends at once. Both girls were shy, but with each other their shyness melted away. They were the same age and of course they had the same interests: music, music, music!

When they weren't rehearsing, the girls had sleepovers at Bey's house. They played Truth or Dare and teased each other – especially Bey – about boys.

"The boys like you so much, Bey! Isn't there anyone you like?"

"That one in the front row last night, in the red T-shirt? He couldn't take his eyes off you!"

"Boys are gross!" Bey replied. "Keep them away from me. Please!"

"You're so lucky, Bey. I wish the boys fancied me as much as they fancy you!"

With Kelly, LaTavia, Ashley, Nina and Nicki, every rehearsal was so much fun. But that didn't stop Beyoncé and her friends taking their music more seriously than ever. Andretta's house was the venue for most of their rehearsals now. She loved to spend time with the girls, who called her "Miss Ann". Miss Ann helped each girl to work on her performance, building her self-confidence.

"Kelly, come forward! The audience will want to see you."

"OK, Miss Ann, I'll try."

"Beyoncé, I love your confidence!"

"Thanks, Miss Ann."

"Nicki, Nina – that looks great! Just get those arms moving a bit quicker."

"Yes, Miss Ann."

"Miss Ann, can we take a break now?" asked LaTavia.

"LaTavia, come on!" cried Bey. "It's not perfect yet. We need to keep going till it's just right!"

"You're working them hard, Beyoncé," laughed Andretta. "OK, one more go. Then some time out, my orders."

Most of Girl's Tyme's concerts were at local shopping malls. Bey and her friends sang to big, excitable crowds of kids and their parents. Usually Ashley was the lead singer, as her voice was so mature and rich. But sometimes Bey would take centre stage.

"Ashley's brilliant," Andretta would say to Lonnie. "But she doesn't have the stage presence that Beyoncé does."

It was true. Beyoncé performed with a style and flair that Ashley didn't have. She connected with the audience in a very special way.

But all the girls were learning fast. They were inspiring each other. When each show was over, Bey and her friends watched tapes of their performance, picking out the bits that needed improvement.

"The middle section isn't as good as the rest," said Bey. "We need new choreography."

"We'll talk to Keith tomorrow," said Kelly. "He'll fix it for us."

"I know what it needs," said Bey. "Let's work on it now. Come on, I'll show you!"

"Nooo!" groaned Nicki. "Tomorrow, please!"

"Tonight," said Bey firmly.

She couldn't help it. Bey lived and breathed music. Girl's Tyme was her life. And although they might grumble sometimes, she knew that the other girls felt the same.

In addition to watching Girl's Tyme on tape, and learning from her mistakes, Bey also studied videos by artists like Michael Jackson and Prince. She looked closely at their performances, making notes on everything. She also listened to older singers like Jackie Wilson, James Brown and Diana Ross. There was so much to learn! And who better to learn from than the biggest superstars of all time...

One day, the group's songwriter, Anthony Moore – or Tony Mo, as everyone called him – had an idea. The girls were rehearsing after school, as usual, when he came in with a stack of notepads and pens.

"Aw, Tony, no! Not more homework!" the girls groaned.

"School's done for the day, Tony."

"I'm not picking up another pen!"

"Nuh-uh."

Tony smiled. "This isn't homework. You girls are going to write some songs!"

The girls grimaced. They were tired. They had already worked hard this evening.

But Tony wasn't taking no for an answer. "Here are your pens and paper, girls. You've got fifteen minutes. I want to see some brilliant lyrics!"

Brilliant lyrics? That was going to be tough! The girls didn't know how Tony wrote the songs they sang. They didn't know how he got his ideas. It seemed like some kind of magic.

"What should we write about?" asked Kelly.

"You can write about anything you like,"

said Tony. "Something that's special to you. Or something that's upset you. Or something that you're scared of. Just write about what you're feeling."

The girls looked at each other. Suddenly they felt self-conscious. Write about themselves? What if Tony laughed at them?

"I'm not going to laugh at you," he said, as if reading their minds.

Beyoncé grabbed her pad and threw herself down on the sofa. She might be confident onstage, but offstage she was still shy. Writing sounded like a good way to express herself. She was excited to give it a try.

There was silence for a few minutes as the girls stared at their blank pages. Then everyone heard a pen start to scribble. The other girls looked up. It was Bey! Of course.

The minutes ticked by and one by one, the other girls left the room. They handed their pads back to Tony.

"We tried," they said apologetically. "We couldn't think of what to say."

But now she'd started, Beyoncé couldn't stop.

Her head was bobbing up and down to an imaginary beat. Now and again she paused, with her pen in the air. Then it went back to the page, scribbling more lines.

Finally, she threw down her pen. She saw with surprise that she'd filled pages and pages. Some lines she could barely read, they were written in such a hurry. Was it good? Or was it rubbish? She had no idea!

Tony Mo appeared in the doorway. "You going to show me?"

Nervously, Bey handed him her pad. "I don't think it's very good," she said. "I just wrote about what I feel. Like you said."

Tony looked at the scribbles. He nodded. "Not bad at all, Bey. There are some great lines here."

"Really?"

"You could get good at this," said Tony. "From now on, every time you think of a line, write it down. Take a notepad everywhere. That's what songwriters do. You never know when and where you might have a great idea!"

Bey liked the sound of that.

"Now, do you want to hear something I've written?" asked Tony. "It's called 'Sunshine'. It's a new song for the group. I think you're going to like it..."

CHAPTER 9

IN THE STUDIO

Two very exciting things had happened, and Andretta couldn't wait to tell the girls. They were rehearsing at Denise and Deborah's studio that evening, and she hurried there as quickly as she could.

"You're going to make your first recording!" Andretta announced. "We're going to a studio in Houston. You'll work with Lonnie and a sound engineer."

The girls jumped up and down with excitement. Recording their songs like proper artists... They'd been dreaming of this for months!

"It's one of the best studios in the city," added Andretta.

"What will we sing?" asked Bey.

"'Sunshine'," said Andretta. "Of course."

Everyone loved Tony Mo's new song: the girls, their parents, Andretta and Lonnie – and, most importantly, their audiences. Once they'd heard the chorus, the crowd would always sing along. It was so upbeat and catchy.

"That's not all though, girls," said Andretta slyly. "There's more."

More?! What could possibly be as exciting as making a recording in a real studio?

"We're going to California!" Andretta said. "I've booked you into a showcase. All the major record labels will be there, looking for new talent."

OK, that *was* even more exciting! The girls whirled each other round the room, whooping and shrieking with joy. Girl's Tyme was getting well known around Houston. But California...! That was *massive*! They knew many of the record companies were based on the West Coast. Maybe this would be their big break.

"We'll all go – you and your parents, me, Lonnie, Keith and Tony Mo," Andretta told them.

Denise and Deborah would stay in Houston to look after business there.

Wow! The girls had never travelled so far. Bey had never even been on a plane. It would be an amazing adventure.

"We'll need to start preparing," said Andretta. "Everything needs to be perfect."

"Everything needs to be perfect," echoed Mathew when he heard the news. "What you girls need... is a bootcamp!"

The girls looked at each other. *A bootcamp? Like in the army?* All six girls were at the Knowleses' having dinner. They had finished rehearsing for the day, but they knew Mathew never stopped thinking about Girl's Tyme and how to achieve the success they all wanted. He was just like Bey – he lived and breathed both music and the group.

"You're already having vocal lessons," Mathew explained. "And Keith is doing choreography. But you need to work on your fitness, too. You need to be able to sing and dance at the same time without getting out of breath."

It was true. The girls sometimes struggled to sing the difficult, quick bits while performing their dance routines. Even professional singers found that hard. But surely rehearsals would give them enough practice? What did Mathew have in mind?

"Jogging!" He smiled. "Jogging while singing. We'll start tomorrow!"

"We?" they asked.

"I'll do it, too. Practise what you preach, girls. That's what I always say."

Bootcamp began the following day, in the Knowleses' back garden. The girls lined up and, instructed by Mathew, began to jog on the spot. *Sing! Jog! Star jumps! Squats! Faster! Go-go-go!*

Beyoncé pulled a face. "You're so embarrassing, Dad!"

"I'm going to call your dad the Drill Sergeant from now on, Bey," puffed LaTavia.

"This is exhausting. I can't take any more!" moaned Nina.

Five-year-old Solange came running out of the

patio doors. "Can I join in, Daddy?" she cried. She began to run wildly around on the grass, her arms whirling like a windmill.

Everyone laughed.

"See, girls?" said Mathew, grinning. "That's the attitude I'm looking for. Come on, Solange. Show them how it's done!"

While Mathew focused on the girls' fitness, Andretta and Tina were thinking about costumes. They needed some eye-catching new outfits for the girls to wear onstage in California.

"Motown," said Tina. "The Jackson 5. That's the look we should go for."

Andretta agreed. They bought sparkly white tuxedo jackets with shoulder pads, silk blouses and bow ties. Then they sewed hundreds of extra sequins onto the costumes so that they would sparkle under the stage lights.

"Wow," said Andretta when they were finished. "These will be the best costumes at the showcase, I guarantee."

"What's our budget?" Tina asked. "I've seen

these amazing glow-in-the-dark boots. Seriously, Andretta. The girls *need* these boots!"

She named the price.

Andretta winced. "We just don't have enough money, Tina, I'm sorry. Not with the plane tickets and hotel rooms as well."

Tina had made up her mind, though. She assembled Bey and her friends, and they went back to the mall. When she asked for a discount on the boots, the store manager said no, but Tina had a back-up plan...

"This is Girl's Tyme," she said, gesturing towards the girls, who were browsing the rails of glamorous clothing. "The boots are for them. Will you give me a discount if they sing outside the store?"

Girl's Tyme were becoming well known in Houston. They had performed in this mall many times and the shoppers loved them. The store manager thought for a moment. A concert would certainly draw in the customers. "OK, we've got a deal. *If* the girls will sing 'Sunshine'..."

Tony's new song had quickly become their signature tune.

"OK, girls," Tina called. "Impromptu concert!"

"Mom!" hissed Bey anxiously. "We haven't got our backing track!"

"We're not dressed for a concert, Miss Tina," said LaTavia, plucking the strap of her dungarees.

"You look just fine, girls, take it from me," insisted Tina. "And you *know* you don't need a backing track. Half the time you practise without any music." She smiled. "Please! For me?"

"For glow-in-the-dark boots, you mean, Mom!" said Bey mischievously. She looked at Ashley, who nodded. Tina was right: they were used to singing *a cappella* – without music. And who cared what they were wearing?!

Ashley led the girls to the front of the store and hit the first note. The others came in immediately and, in seconds, their harmonies were floating through the mall. The first passer-by, an elderly gentleman, looked surprised. The second, a dad with two young kids, stopped to listen. The little kids began to dance, mimicking the girls' routine as best they could. A young couple stopped, then a group of teens. Tina winked at Bey. It was working!

Almost every passer-by stopped to listen, and plenty of them wandered into the store, humming the music as they went.

The girls grinned at each other. This unexpected concert was the best fun ever. They loved seeing the surprise and pleasure on the faces of the shoppers. It felt like a party!

"You really earned those boots," said Tina once the girls had sung the final song.

Bey grinned. She knew that every time they wore the amazing glow-in-the-dark boots, they would remember the equally amazing store-front concert.

In between bootcamp, costume fittings, vocal coaching and dance practice, Andretta and Lonnie took Bey and the girls to the recording studio.

"This will be the first time of many," said Lonnie, smiling. "You'll get used to this place."

Each girl took a turn to sit with Lonnie in the recording booth, singing her part in front of a microphone, with large headphones over her ears. Lonnie sat in front of a huge, slanting desk, adjusting the audio levels, listening and pressing buttons. The other girls waited outside, watching through the glass window and making faces.

When it was Beyoncé's turn, she was full of questions. Patiently, Lonnie explained everything he was doing. Bey's face glowed with pleasure as she stared at the recording desk, listening and asking more questions. So this was how songs were made! Somehow, Bey felt like she belonged here. She loved singing the songs – anywhere, everywhere – but this was a new excitement. This desk controlled how the music sounded. It was so complicated... but she wanted to understand all of it. One day, she wanted to be able to do what Lonnie did so easily!

CHAPTER 10

CALIFORNIA

Bey had never been on a plane, and neither had Mathew or Tina. It was almost impossible for the girls – and their parents – to contain their excitement. As the plane swept into the sky, the group burst into whoops of delight – to the amusement of the other passengers, mostly business people.

By the time they landed in California, four hours later, Bey's excitement had turned into nerves. She was silent as they travelled by taxi to the hotel.

"What's wrong, sweetheart?" Mathew asked her.

"What if I forget the words, Papa?" she whispered.

She wasn't alone in feeling anxious. Kelly was worried about tripping over. LaTavia worried about sneezing or getting a cough. But forgetting the lyrics was always the thing that worried Beyoncé the most.

"If you can't remember the actual words, make some up," suggested Mathew. "No one will know. You're always inventing lyrics. The new ones will probably be just as good as the old ones!"

That made Bey laugh. "Don't forget Tony Mo – he'll know if I don't sing the right words!"

"I'll be there in the front row," her dad reminded her. "If you get nervous, look at me and I'll send some courage your way."

"I love you, Papa," said Beyoncé.

"I love you too, Bey. You make me the proudest dad in the world."

The showcase was the next evening. In their new costumes, with hair and make-up done by Tina, the girls looked like they had just stepped out of a music video.

"You look like professional singers," Andretta told them as they waited backstage to go on.

"I love this outfit!" said Bey. Wearing the sparkly jacket and trousers, she felt like her hero, Michael

Jackson. And she wasn't nearly as nervous as she'd feared – not with her friends around her.

"Time to go. Break a leg!" whispered Andretta.

It was one of the best performances Girl's Tyme had ever given. They oozed confidence. Soon, the audience were clapping along, with their hands in the air. Then, to close their show, the girls had a dance-off, live onstage. The audience went wild!

Finally, LaTavia delivered a rap, thanking their parents.

"And special thanks to Andretta, Lonnie and Tony Mo!" added Bey, leaning into the microphone.

The audience were on their feet, cheering and clapping. And – wait – was that Mathew coming onto the stage? In her surprise, Bey almost dropped the mic. Was her dad going to sing as well?!

No – phew! In his hand, Mathew held a bunch of red roses. He presented one to each girl: Beyoncé, Kelly, LaTavia, Ashley, Nicki and Nina. They had done it. They had given the performance of their lives!

It wasn't long before Andretta had good news to share. The Plant Studios in San Francisco – one of the most famous recording studios in America – wanted to record Girl's Tyme. Bey gasped in awe when she heard the names of the stars who had recorded there: Stevie Wonder, Prince, Fleetwood Mac... the list went on and on.

But the other girls were confused. "We just made a recording, here in Houston. Can't we give them that?"

"Well, each studio likes to make their own recording," said Andretta, "using their own equipment and sound engineer. Then they send that to the record label."

Bey nodded. Mathew had explained this to her already. The process seemed complicated, but if that was how it worked...

However, there was disappointing news for Kelly and LaTavia. There wasn't enough money to send all four girls to San Francisco to make the recording. Only Beyoncé and Ashley would be going – and without their parents.

"Beyoncé's only ten!" said Tina anxiously. "She's too young."

"They'll be fine," Ashley's mum reassured her.

"They're not babies any more. Plus, Andretta and Keith will be travelling with them."

So it was settled. Beyoncé and Ashley would travel almost two thousand miles to San Francisco. The girls would be on their own for the first time ever.

Tina sighed. Then smiled. Her little Bey was growing up fast!

A surprise awaited the girls as they emerged from the arrivals gate.

"A limo!" squealed Ashley. "For us?!"

Waiting at the kerb was a white stretch limo, with a chauffeur at the wheel. Bey gasped. "I *wish* Kelly and LaTavia were here! We must be dreaming, right?"

The girls scrambled in, followed by Andretta and Keith. The seats were made of white leather and there was even a screen playing MTV.

"You think this is luxury, girls?" said Andretta. "Wait till you see where we're going!"

The chauffeur drove them slowly through the streets of San Francisco till they reached a huge hotel, nestled on the hillside. The Claremont Hotel. Five stars. It looked like an enormous white palace, the sort owned by a princess in a fairy tale. Bey and Ashley squeezed each other's hands. Was this what being a singer was like? It seemed to them like the best job in the world!

Recording began the next day. Bey and Ashley took it in turns to sing 'Sunshine', sitting in the booth, each singing their own parts, plus Kelly and LaTavia's. Then they tried a new song that Tony Mo had written for them. It was called 'Blue Velvet'. It was fast, with lots of difficult rhythms.

"This song is *really* complicated!" moaned Ashley, who was singing lead vocals. "I'm never going to get it."

"Try again," said Lonnie. "Slower this time. You can do it."

But Ashley couldn't master the tricky, irregular beat. "It's too hard," she said. "I need to stop."

"Can I try?" asked Bey.

Lonnie nodded. He had been hoping to use Ashley's richer voice for the lead. But if Beyoncé could learn the notes more easily, he would happily let her take over.

"Go for it," he told her.

And she did. To Lonnie's astonishment, Bey mastered the tune and the rhythm on the first try. "Wow, Bey. How did you do that so quickly?"

"I just listened, I guess," Bey told him. "It didn't seem that hard."

"Why don't you sing the backing vocals now?" Lonnie suggested.

Ashley waited outside the recording booth while Bey continued to sing. She was so relieved to be out of the spotlight, no longer struggling with the difficult song, that she didn't notice her friend had recorded the whole song by herself.

CHAPTER 11

STAR SEARCH

Ashley's parents had definitely noticed that their daughter hadn't sung!

Back in Houston, the girls and their parents and managers had gathered together to listen to the finished recording.

"What's going on here?" Ashley's parents asked Lonnie angrily. "We can only hear Beyoncé. Where's Ashley?"

It was true. And it wasn't only 'Blue Velvet' where Beyoncé was singing all the parts. Ashley's parents were dismayed to find that their daughter was hardly singing on any of the songs.

Lonnie had a simple explanation. "Beyoncé's a star in the making," he told them. "If we feature her more, Girl's Tyme has a better chance of succeeding."

Lonnie revealed that while they had been recording, a lot of record executives had been interested in Beyoncé. "There's a buzz around her," he told them.

The parents understood, even Ashley's parents – eventually. They all wanted the group to secure a record deal. If this was the way to do it, they would support it.

There was another change coming, too. Mathew had requested to co-manage the group alongside Andretta. He cared deeply about the girls and the group.

"We need to take them to the next level," he told the other parents. "I know how to do it." The other parents could see how determined he was. They knew he was a successful salesperson. They agreed.

"I know what this means," joked LaTavia. "More bootcamp!"

Mathew's first idea was to build a stage in the backyard of the Knowleses' house. If the girls could practise on an actual stage, it would help their performances. He also bought a sound machine and mics. Bey and her friends continued to work with their vocal teacher, while Mathew helped them to polish their performances.

Then another big change happened. Kelly's mum decided to move back to Atlanta.

Kelly cried when she found out – and so did Bey. Kelly was her best friend. They were like sisters.

Kelly's family was from Atlanta, but she had lived in Houston since she was six. Houston was her home. She knew no one in Atlanta. She would have to leave the group. And her friends.

But Kelly's mum had made her decision. There was no changing her mind. Kelly had tried!

Then Mathew and Tina offered a solution. Kelly could come and live with them. She spent so much time at their house anyway, they said. They thought of her as a daughter.

Bey and Kelly were delighted. Living with a best friend – it was a dream come true. Bey was so proud of her generous, caring parents. They had made

Kelly happy – and they had made Bey happy, too.

And now there was even more time to work on their music together!

One of Bey and Kelly's favourite things to do was to watch *Star Search* with the rest of the family on a Saturday night. *Star Search* was a reality TV show featuring amateur singers from all over America, who were trying to win fame and fortune. The girls loved to watch the acts and rate their performances. They loved the drama, too: every Saturday night, a new act would try to beat the existing champions, competing head to head for the judges' votes. The loser would leave the show. It was so tense!

And now it was their turn.

Andretta and Mathew had booked Girl's Tyme to appear on the show!

Live TV... The girls couldn't stop talking about it. Lots of pop stars had been discovered on *Star Search* – Christina Aguilera, Usher, Britney Spears... It was an amazing opportunity, the most exciting thing they had ever done.

"I'm sooo nervous!" shrieked Kelly.

"What if we fall off the stage?!" giggled LaTavia.

"Or forget the words," added Bey, as she always did.

Meanwhile, the grown-ups were discussing the show, too. By now, the girls had many, many songs to choose from. But which was the best for live TV?

"They should sing 'Boyfriend'," said Andretta.

"With Beyoncé and Ashley on lead vocals," said Keith. "Great idea."

"I disagree. We should put Beyoncé on lead," said Lonnie. "Just her. She's the star."

"They're *all* stars," said Andretta firmly.

"It needs to be Beyoncé," said Mathew. "That's what's going to win the competition. Remember California..."

"Let's go with 'That's the Way It Is in My City'," said Lonnie. "Beyoncé singing, LaTavia and Ashley rapping."

"C'mon, the rap section only lasts a few seconds!" said Tony Mo. "It's only fair to let all the girls have their moment."

"They'll get their moment. But first we've got to win."

Tony, Andretta and Keith looked at each other. But Mathew and Lonnie wouldn't be budged. They had decided, and that was that.

It was Beyoncé who would be centre stage on *Star Search*.

On the night that Girl's Tyme appeared on *Star Search*, the reigning champions were a rock group called Skeleton Crew. All the band members were adults. They were all at least fifteen years older than Beyoncé and her friends.

Bey and the girls watched nervously from backstage. They could see how polished the act was. She could hear the studio crowd going wild. If the judges loved this, they weren't going to like Girl's Tyme at all. The two acts couldn't be more different.

Mathew leaned in to give his daughter a hug. "Like I always say," he whispered, "do your—"

"Do your best and let the audience do the rest," finished Bey. "Thanks, Dad!"

As Skeleton Crew strode offstage, the lights went low. The host's voice boomed out: *"Welcome*

Beyoncé, LaTavia, Nina, Nicki, Kelly and Ashley, the hip-hop, rapping... Girl's Tyme!"

The girls ran on, six small figures in their bright, co-ordinating outfits. LaTavia bounced to the centre of the stage, launching confidently into her rap section. Then Beyoncé gracefully crossed the stage to take up the melody. Behind her, Kelly and Ashley sang backing vocals, while Nina and Nicki flung themselves into the dance routine.

"They're not doing badly," Lonnie whispered to Keith backstage. "But I don't think it's good enough."

"We should have gone with 'Boyfriend'," replied Keith. "That song makes them sparkle. I have a bad feeling about this..."

It seemed only seconds before the song was finished.

The host's voice spoke again. *"The judges have awarded Skeleton Crew four stars. And they've given our challengers, Girl's Tyme, three stars."*

It was over, as quickly as that.

Beyoncé and the girls forced themselves to

smile while Skeleton Crew waved gratefully to the crowd. Then the lights went down.

Girl's Tyme had never lost anything before. It was all new – and it did *not* feel good.

CHAPTER 12

MISTAKES

The next morning, the girls and their parents met in Lonnie's hotel room. Lonnie was holding a videotape of the performance. Bey and her friends looked at each other nervously. His face was stern. This was not going to be fun.

Everyone gathered round the TV, and Lonnie ran the tape.

"Kelly," he said, "you made *way* too many mistakes." He pressed pause and gestured at the screen. "You see that? You're clearly out of time with the others. It's not good enough."

Kelly burst into tears. "I'm sorry," she sobbed. "It's all my fault!"

Bey put her arms around her friend.

"It's OK. It's OK," she whispered. "It's OK."

"You *all* made mistakes," said Mathew, looking round the group. "It's messy. Every single one of you needs to do better."

"Much better," added Lonnie.

One by one, the girls began to cry. Their successes in Houston seemed so far away, like a dream. A record deal? How could that possibly happen now? The whole country had seen them fail on live TV!

Only Beyoncé wasn't crying. She looked her dad in the eye and nodded. "We *can* do better. I know we can. We mustn't give up."

But the other girls weren't listening.

Girl's Tyme had never failed before. They didn't know what to do with this unexpected defeat.

Kelly was sobbing wildly into a pillow. "I'm the reason we lost," she howled. "I ruined it!"

"OK, that's enough!" Tina pushed past Mathew and sank onto the bed beside her. "It is not your fault," she said gently, pulling Kelly into her arms. "You did your best. All of you."

Turning to Mathew and Lonnie, she said, "Go easy on them. They're so young!"

Lonnie sighed. She was right. Of course she was.

"*Star Search* is not the end of the world," Tina continued. "It's done, and now you kids are going to have some fun. We're going to Disneyland!"

Bey looked at her with surprise. "But you said we could only go to Disneyland if we won."

"C'mon, do you really think we'd do that to you!" said Tina. She wiped Kelly's eyes and gave her another hug. "You all worked so hard. Win or lose, you deserve a good time."

Star Search had been disappointing for everyone. By the time the group arrived back in Houston, Mathew had taken the time to do some thinking.

"Some incredible things have happened over the past few years," he said to Tina. "But the girls still need a record deal."

Tina agreed. Bey and her friends had so much talent. It was frustrating that things weren't moving more quickly.

"What can we do?" she asked. "Andretta is doing her best."

"I want to manage the group full-time," Mathew

told her. "I'll take a course in show business management, learn the ropes."

Tina gulped. "You mean you would leave your job?"

Mathew nodded. "Things may be difficult for a while, but this is the right thing to do." He reminded her of how poor his own family had been. He had grown up with nothing. "But I've never let it hold me back," he said. "I worked and worked until I succeeded. Now my daughter has a dream and I want to help her make it come true."

Tina was nervous. Only the income from her hair salon to support the family? Mathew's job was very well paid. They lived in a large house and had two cars. Their daughters had grown up without having to worry about money...

But Tina had also grown up with very little. She had built up her salon from nothing, and now it was a thriving business. She was as determined as Mathew to succeed. Maybe everything would be OK, after all.

She nodded. "Bey wants to be a singer more than anything in the world. If we can help her, we should."

CHAPTER 13

ASHLEY

"Where's Ashley? It's not like her to be late to rehearsal."

Bey and the girls were in the Knowleses' family room, sprawled on the sofa. They'd planned to rehearse some songs in which Ashley was the lead vocalist. There wasn't much point starting without her.

"Has she called, Mom?" asked Bey, although she knew the answer already.

Minutes turned into hours. Still the telephone didn't ring.

"Something's up," said Kelly. "She wouldn't just not contact us."

A car pulled up outside. The girls rushed to the door. But it wasn't Ashley; it was Andretta.

"She knows something," whispered Bey. "Look at her face."

Andretta's expression was grim. Her news surprised all the girls. "Ashley has left Girl's Tyme. Her parents have pulled her out."

It took a moment for the news to sink in. Ashley? No longer part of the group? The girls stared at each other in silence. Then, suddenly, the questions tumbled out:

"Why? What happened?"

"Is she OK?"

"Did her parents make her leave?"

"Is she joining another group?"

Mathew raised his hand for silence.

"That's enough," he said. "She's gone and that's that."

"But how come she didn't tell us?" exclaimed Bey. "I'm calling her."

"No, you're not!" said Mathew. "This is complicated. Ashley is doing her thing and you're doing your thing."

"I want to know what's going on!" Bey cried.

"I said NO!" Mathew fixed his daughter with

a stern look. Then his gaze travelled around the room. "That goes for the rest of you, too."

"It's about *Star Search*, I know it," whispered Bey to Kelly, once her dad had left the room.

"All I know is that I want to stay in the group," said Kelly. "Whatever it takes."

Bey hugged her. They had each other. That was the most important thing.

February came round. Finally, the dreaded episode of *Star Search* was shown on national TV. Usually Bey and Kelly looked forward to Saturday night – but not this time.

"I can't watch," said Kelly to Bey. "I wish it had never happened."

"Me too. Think of all the people who will be watching us!"

The girls cringed. Everyone they knew watched *Star Search*. Their classmates. Their teachers. The kids they knew at church. The women who had their hair done at Tina's salon.

Beyoncé smiled at her friend. "We'll get past it. I know we will."

All the girls were determined to work hard. It had been strange rehearsing without Ashley. It was like missing a family member. But they could do it – they had to.

Still, the girls couldn't help wondering what Ashley was doing. None of the girls saw her now. They didn't call her, either. Bey and her friends knew better than to defy Mathew when he said no. None of their parents ever mentioned Ashley. They had never explained why she left. Had she wanted to go? Had Mathew kicked her out?

But there were other things to think about, too. There was a new girl in the group. Her name was LeToya Luckett and Bey knew her from school. She had a lovely soprano voice. She and LaTavia sang the harmonies, while Kelly was the second lead vocalist alongside Bey.

And there was more change coming...

Mathew had made another decision. They needed to move on from *Star Search* and hope that the public would forget about that losing performance. They needed a new name. Something to replace Girl's Tyme. Something fresh...

Somethin' Fresh – that was it!

As easily as that, the group had a new name. A new identity.

At least, they did for a bit. It wasn't long before Mathew and the group's producer, Daryl, had another idea.

Goodbye, Somethin' Fresh. Hello, The Dolls!

"Because they look just like little dolls when they're up on that stage," said Daryl.

"Perfect," said Mathew.

There was exciting news, too: The Dolls would be singing at a showcase in Atlanta. All the major record companies would be there.

The girls were rehearsing harder than ever. They sang, danced and exercised for up to twelve hours a day. They were exhausted. But Bey kept the girls motivated. Their dream was within their grasp. They had to keep going...

"Just one more time! We can do it even better. Let's get it right, *then* we can rest."

"Bey, you're as bad as the Drill Sergeant," LaTavia groaned.

Bey grinned. She was used to the girls calling her "Mom" when she tried to take care of them, but being compared to Mathew was a new joke. She supposed she did have plenty in common with her dad, too!

"There's someone at the door!" cried Kelly.

The girls had travelled to Atlanta. Their producer, Daryl, who had organised the showcase, was letting them rehearse in his house. But the girls were tired of practising. They jumped at any excuse to stop rehearsing for a few minutes – even if it was only a delivery person.

"Beat you down there!"

"Unlikely!"

The girls scrambled down the stairs and LeToya flung open the front door.

A handsome teen in a baseball cap was standing on the step.

Kelly gasped.

"It's Usher," she hissed.

The girls exchanged looks. They didn't need to be told. Usher was only sixteen, but he was famous all over the world. His face was everywhere...

... and now he was on their doorstep!

Even confident LaTavia was lost for words.

"You girls going to let me in?" he asked.

The girls shuffled out of the way.

"Daryl's my producer," Usher explained. "I hang out here all the time. Who are you?"

Bey spoke up. "We're The Dolls." She hesitated. She couldn't get used to the new name. It just didn't sound right. "We're from Houston."

"So what do you think of Atlanta, Dolls?"

"We haven't had time to see it," said LaTavia. "Not with the Drill Sergeant on our backs all the time," she laughed. "And Beyoncé, too!"

"We're rehearsing for a showcase," explained Kelly.

"Then I need to show you around." Usher smiled. "Don't worry. I'll speak to your manager, the Drill Sergeant."

"That's my dad," added Bey.

"I can speak to him, too."

"No, Bey's dad manages us," explained LeToya. "It's the same person."

Usher smiled. "Never heard that one. But, OK. Let's go find him."

Charmed by Usher, Mathew gave the girls the afternoon off. "This is going to be a whistle-stop tour," Usher warned them. "Atlanta is *big*."

The first stop was Usher's own neighbourhood. Then he whisked them around the sights: the world's largest indoor aquarium; Piedmont Park; Varsity, the largest drive-in restaurant in the world; the Georgia State Capitol and, finally, 501 Auburn Avenue, the house where Dr Martin Luther King Jr was born, and the Ebenezer Baptist Church where he preached.

"His grave is in the Memorial Park," explained Usher. "Just over there."

The girls were silent. They were standing right in front of the house where Dr Martin Luther King had lived! He had played in that yard as a child. He had looked out of those windows. He had run along the pavement they were standing on. It was almost impossible to imagine...

"There's just one more thing you should see,"

said Usher. "The downtown skyline at sunset."

Bey looked nervously at her watch. "It's getting late. Tomorrow is our big chance, girls. We can't be tired."

"OK, Mom," the five girls chorused.

Bey smiled – and Usher smiled, too. "It won't take long, I promise. It'll be worth it," he said.

The pink-and-gold sunset and glittering skyscrapers were beautiful, just as Usher had promised. The girls all agreed: Atlanta was amazing. They would come back here as soon as they could. And the scenery was only one of the attractions...

"I have *such* a crush on Usher!" whispered Kelly to Bey.

"Me too," Bey giggled.

Beyoncé was so happy. She was on an extraordinary journey with five fantastic friends – and an Atlanta sunset with Usher was the cherry on the cake.

Bey needn't have worried. The girls were at their best when the showcase came round the next evening. Backstage, they were fizzing with excitement – and as soon as they stepped out onto the stage, they dazzled the audience with their talent. Bey felt like she was singing from up in the clouds.

"I'm so proud of you," said Andretta afterwards. "That was magical."

"It felt amazing," Bey told her.

"Let's hope the record companies feel the same," said Andretta. "I don't think The Dolls have ever sung better."

Bey grimaced. "The Dolls. It just doesn't sound right for us."

"You don't like the name? Me neither," admitted Andretta. "But..."

Bey raised an eyebrow. They both knew how hard it was to change Mathew's mind once he'd decided on something. His determination was one of the things Bey loved so much about him.

But still, she could never love 'The Dolls'!

CHAPTER 14

A DEAL

"Kelly Rowland and Beyoncé Knowles, please come to the principal's office."

The announcement was made over the tannoy, broadcast across the whole school. Kelly and Bey looked at each other in alarm.

"What did we do?" whispered Kelly.

They hurried to the principal's office.

"It must be bad," said Bey. "I'm so nervous."

"You go first." Kelly nudged her friend as they reached the door.

Bey turned the handle and the two girls stumbled into the office. Mathew was there with the school principal. They weren't frowning, though, they were smiling. Grinning, in fact. Bey felt her stomach do an anxious somersault. What on earth was going on?

Then Mathew's voice filled the room: "Girls, you've got a record deal! We're going back to Atlanta. Bey, Kelly, you've got a deal. It's happening at last!"

Bey and Kelly's screams were in perfect synch – and so loud the whole school must have heard them. The principal winced, and then smiled.

"Well done, girls. We're right behind you."

"We did it, Kelly!" cried Bey, embracing her best friend.

Mathew hugged them both. "It's not done yet. You've got a lot of hard work ahead of you."

Bey grinned. She understood. She would work as hard as she needed to.

"You'll have to quit school, I'm afraid. We'll get you a tutor," said Mathew. "And there's just one other thing..."

"You're kidding!" said LaTavia when she heard the news. Her eyes were wide with panic. "They only want four of us?"

The whole group was assembled in Andretta's dining room, sitting round the large table.

"It's the record label," Andretta explained. "They've made up their mind. They say six is too many. They want Beyoncé, Kelly and LeToya. Nina, Nicki and LaTavia, you're going to have to audition for the fourth place. There's nothing I can do, girls. I'm so sorry."

"But they can't break us up like this," said Kelly. "It's our group!"

Bey glanced at Andretta, whose kind face crumpled as she looked round the table at the girls she loved.

"They *can* do it," said Bey grimly. "They can do whatever they want."

"It's not fair," cried Kelly.

"That's show business, girls," said Andretta. "Nothing is fair. Nicki, Nina, LaTavia – you're going to work with a vocal coach to prepare. The audition is next week. Good luck, all of you. I wish things were different, I really do."

Beyoncé, Kelly and LeToya watched nervously as

the other girls prepared for their audition. They could imagine how upset their friends must be. Everyone had worked so hard to get here! They were relieved it wasn't them who had to sing for a place in the group. But they couldn't help feeling guilty.

LeToya said what they all were feeling. "This sucks."

"I can't believe the group is going to be broken up," said Kelly.

The girls agreed.

Not only were the other girls competing as friends, but they were also family. Nina and Nicki were sisters, and LaTavia was their cousin.

"It must feel so bad," sighed Bey.

The week went by painfully slowly, but eventually the day of the audition came. Nicki, Nina and LaTavia wished each other good luck. All three girls had their strengths. They were all talented singers.

In the end, it was LaTavia who won the final place in the group. Her rapping skills were the best of all the girls and her vocals were strong, too. Nicki and Nina hugged her, and Andretta flung her arms round the three of them.

"You're *all* amazing in my eyes," she told them.

"It happened to Ashley. Now it's happening to us," said Nina.

Beyoncé, Kelly, LaTavia and LeToya said sad goodbyes to the two sisters.

"Goodbye, Nicki. Goodbye, Nina. We love you."

"Good luck, all of you," said Nicki and Nina. "We love you, too."

It seemed to Bey that the fun might be over this time. It had been tough starting again without Ashley, but starting again without Nicki and Nina felt so much worse. Bey had known them since she was nine, when they had all auditioned for Denise and Deborah's show. It was so sad to see her old friends leave. Suddenly, everything the group did felt like hard work.

And it wasn't only in the rehearsal room that things were gloomy. By now, Mathew had finished his course in show business management and was managing the group full-time. Bey could see how hard he was working. When he wasn't rehearsing with the Dolls, he was on the phone or sending emails in his office. Bey knew her parents were worried about money. Their big, beautiful house, with all its happy memories, had been sold. For months, the Knowleses had been spending less and less time together as a family.

Eventually, Mathew and Tina split up. Bey had seen it coming, but still it felt like their family had been ripped apart. A heavy weight had fallen on her shoulders and wouldn't shift. Writing about her unhappiness, in songs, didn't seem to help, either.

Finally, a few months later, the record label dropped The Dolls. They would not be releasing a record. It seemed as though all that hard work had been for nothing.

Tina and the girls moved into a new two-bed apartment, without Mathew. Bey and Kelly shared a room. Solange shared with Tina. After their huge house with its big garden and the amazing wooden stage that Mathew had made, it seemed so small and cramped.

Bey spent hours alone in her room.

Mathew and Andretta did their best to distract Bey and Kelly. The daily rehearsals continued. Tony Mo still encouraged them to write songs. They still did concerts and watched the tapes back afterwards, striving to improve their performance each time.

But it was hard to keep believing in their dream.

There was a glimpse of a silver lining, though. A new production company was interested in the group. Perhaps it was a good omen that they had changed their name. Mathew had discovered another band called The Dolls, so he and Andretta chose 'Destiny' – like the group Deborah and Denise had managed alongside Girl's Tyme. The girls were pleased. No one had liked 'The Dolls'.

This time, the girls had to travel to Oakland, California, to make their recording. They knew it was dangerous to get their hopes up, after what happened last time. But a few weeks later, when Mathew got a call from an executive at Columbia Records, Teresa LaBarbera Whites, inviting the girls to perform at the Columbia Records office in New York, it was impossible not to feel excited again.

Teresa explained to Mathew that she had heard the girls sing a few years before, in Houston. What had they been called? Girl's Tyme, that was it! She had liked their sound and the energy of their performance. She remembered a tall, charismatic girl singing lead vocals.

"That was my daughter, Beyoncé," Mathew said proudly.

"They sound like proper artists now," said Teresa. "I can't wait to hear them live."

So, a few days later, Bey and her friends were crammed into a boardroom at the Columbia Records office in New York. They had performed in front of thousands of people, but nothing had *ever* been as nerve-wracking as this. An audience of fans would clap and cheer. This audience, dressed in dark suits, did not react at all. Their faces were blank. Did they like the music? If they did, they seemed determined not to show it.

Bey tried to pretend that she was onstage, with a sea of fans in front of her. She smiled at the other girls, encouraging them. They had to give their best performances. They had to pretend they were having fun!

Finally, it was over. The faces around the room still showed nothing. No one smiled. No one clapped. Mathew led them out of the room.

"You did well," he whispered. "They liked you."

Really? It didn't seem that way!

CHAPTER 15

DESTINY'S CHILD

"Girls! Come here, I've got something for you."

Beyoncé, Kelly, LeToya and LaTavia were hanging out at Headliners one afternoon, when Mathew appeared out of the blue. The salon was busy. Tina looked up from her client and frowned. He always had to choose the busiest possible moment to show up!

Mathew held out four envelopes, one for each of the girls. They were branded with the familiar Luby's cafeteria logo. Bey and her family always ate lunch there after church on a Sunday.

"Luby's!" said Bey, taking the envelope. "Wow – thanks, Dad."

"Thanks, Mr Knowles!"

"Yeah, thank you, Mr Knowles. Luby's is the best."

"Well, open them!" said Mathew.

"They're gift certificates, right?"

"I could just eat some Luby's fries right now..."

"Just open the envelopes!"

The girls tore open their envelopes. But the logo at the top of the paper wasn't Luby's...

"*Columbia!*" shrieked Bey. "Dad! Is this what I think it is?!"

"You've each got a contract," said Mathew. "Right there in your hands."

"A contract! Oh. My. God."

"With Columbia! We've done it!"

"For real!"

Tina turned to the lady in the chair, a new client.

"My girl is going to be famous!" she squealed. She could barely keep from dancing round the room.

"So that's what the racket is about." The girls were whooping and squealing, whirling each other round the salon. The woman smiled. She reached out to touch Bey's arm as she flew past. "What's your name, honey?"

"Beyoncé, ma'am."

"Beyoncé. I'll be sure to remember that."

Most of the women in the salon knew Tina's daughter and the other members of the group. They had been practising here for years. Tina's clients were their first audience. After they finished singing, Tina would hand the girls a broom so they could sweep up the hair on the floor!

The women were delighted at the news.

"I always knew you'd make it," one of the regulars told Bey.

"Oh, honey, that's wonderful."

"Amazing."

"Just make sure you keep your feet on the ground!"

For a half hour, Headliners was the centre of the universe, and the girls already felt like stars.

"Really? We have to change our name *again*?" Kelly burst out laughing.

"We must be cursed or something," said LaTavia. "Are there any band names left?"

"We've got no choice," explained Beyoncé.

Columbia Records already had a group called Alton McClain and Destiny. It was too close.

But Tina had an idea:

"How about Destiny's *Child*?"

"I kinda like it," said Bey. "Destiny's Child. DC. It's got a ring to it."

"You know what they say – fourth time lucky," joked Kelly.

"No one says that," laughed LeToya. "But the name is cool!"

The group were spending more time together than ever. They rehearsed together, studied together, ate together, went to the gym together, even went to church together.

"It's lucky we get along, right?" said Kelly.

"It's not like we have time to have any other friends!"

"What about Lyndall, Bey? What's going on with you two?"

"Aw, no. I don't want to talk about him."

"You never tell us anything, Beyoncé Knowles!"

Beyoncé had first met Lyndall Locke when she

was twelve. He went to the same church as Kelly. Now they were girlfriend and boyfriend. Lyndall had only just found out Bey was a singer. She always liked to keep her music a secret. But the more concerts that Destiny's Child performed, the more fans they gained. It was getting harder and harder for shy Bey to keep her singing hidden.

"So if you had to choose, Bey. Music or Lyndall?" said Kelly.

"C'mon, dumb question!"

All the girls knew the answer. They had never met anyone as determined to follow her dream as Beyoncé. Destiny's Child was her whole life.

"You get it, right?" Bey smiled.

They did. The girls all knew that they would make the same choice. Right now, a singing career felt within their grasp. It was only a matter of time.

CHAPTER 16

BACK IN THE STUDIO

"I don't have to sing the lead all the time, you know!"

Bey frowned at the group's new producer, D'wayne Wiggins. Destiny's Child were in the studio, recording their first album. Beyoncé and D'wayne were in the recording booth, while the other girls sat patiently on the other side of the glass.

"This part would be good for Kelly," added Bey. "Don't you think?"

"Please, D'wayne!" called Kelly from the other side of the partition. "Let me get in there and sing."

By now, the girls were pros. They had been in studios many times before. Bey, in particular, understood lots about the technical side of the production. She knew what sounded good – and how to make it happen.

She also knew how frustrated her best friend was feeling, waiting for hours just to record a few seconds of backing vocals.

D'wayne scratched his head.

"The thing is, Bey, this is what Mathew wants. If you sing all the lead vocals, the sound is consistent and recognisable. Fans will know immediately that it's Destiny's Child."

"But Dad's not here, D'wayne," said Bey firmly.

"True, but—"

"Kelly's going to do it. End of."

D'wayne smiled. Beyoncé could be as stubborn as her father. He knew she was shy when she wasn't performing, but she certainly wasn't like that in the studio. This was Bey's territory. She was in control and knew how to get what she wanted.

He nodded. It was only fair to let the girls share the limelight. "Come on then, Kelly. Show us what you've got."

Bey's skills were growing with every recording session. Her voice was getting stronger and richer.

So was her knowledge of music and she was learning how to create different sounds with her voice.

She was also a leader, motivating the other girls. She worked out the parts that suited their voices and coached them to give their best performances. D'wayne could hardly believe she was only fifteen.

"You sound great, Kelly," said Bey. "But why don't you try it like this?" She demonstrated for her friend.

Kelly did sound great. Her voice was clear and full of power.

But somehow it was always Beyoncé who stole the show.

Destiny's Child was riding high, but not everyone around them was able to enjoy the journey.

Over the past few years, Bey and the group had seen Andretta getting weaker and weaker. Andretta suffered from a disease called Lupus. For years, it had caused her pain and tiredness. As her girls were racing towards success, Andretta was declining rapidly.

Eventually, Andretta died in the Park Plaza

Hospital, Houston. It was the same hospital Beyoncé had been born in fifteen years before. Beyoncé knew how sick Andretta had been, but losing her was more painful than anything she had ever experienced. She loved Andretta deeply, and, in return, Andretta loved her like a daughter. Sitting next to Tina and Mathew at the funeral, Bey wept and wept. Andretta had been a wise, loyal, determined woman. The grieving fifteen-year-old knew how much she owed her mentor.

"I'm going to make her proud," whispered Bey to Tina. "You'll see."

If only Andretta had lived a few months longer. She would have seen what she had been dreaming of for so long: Destiny's Child were releasing their very first song. The track was called 'Killing Time'. It was not coming out as a single. Instead, it featured on the soundtrack of a new film, *Men in Black*, starring Will Smith.

D'wayne was nervous. Was releasing the song on a movie soundtrack the right thing to do? 'Killing Time' was an amazing song. A love song. Beyoncé poured all her emotion into the lead vocals. The other girls sang beautiful harmonies. D'wayne was so proud of what they had achieved. But what if the film did badly? Their brilliant track would be wasted. He couldn't bear to see the group fail – again.

But he needn't have worried.

Men in Black was a huge success. All across the world, audiences flocked to see it. The soundtrack album went to number one in the charts. It stayed there for two weeks, eventually selling three million copies.

So many people had worked so hard for this – D'wayne, Lonnie, Tony Mo, Denise and Deborah, Keith, Mathew and Tina. They were all so proud of their girls.

They knew how proud Andretta would have been, too.

Beyoncé and Destiny's Child were off to an epic start.

CHAPTER 17

NO, NO, NO

Beyoncé stared in mock disbelief as a shining red Mustang pulled up outside her house and her boyfriend, Lyndall Locke, got out. He was dressed in a white bow tie and tuxedo.

"You ready for the prom?" he asked.

"Is that really you?!"

"It's me, baby. The Mustang's rented. Obviously."

"Obviously." Beyoncé smiled.

"You look incredible, Bey."

"My mom made the dress," said Beyoncé, striking a pose in the white halterneck gown. "Do you like it? Kind of a Sixties vibe."

Like it? Bey was the most gorgeous girl Lyndall had ever seen.

"No one's going to have a more beautiful prom date than me," he said.

"And good company too, yeah?"

Lyndall laughed. He knew Beyoncé was about far more than her looks. Bey might be shy, but no one would ever get away with calling her "just a pretty girl".

Bey had never been to a prom before. Mathew and Tina had taken Beyoncé and Kelly out of school. Their schedule of rehearsing, recording and performing made regular classes impossible. Instead, they were studying at home. This was Bey's only chance to experience what other kids took for granted.

"I'm not going to know anyone, you know," she told Lyndall.

"You know me. Surely that's enough!" he joked. "Anyway, soon everyone's going to know *you*."

Bey smiled. Who knew what the future held for Destiny's Child? Their first proper single, 'No, No, No', was coming out any day now. But there had been so many ups and downs. This time Beyoncé knew she had to be cautious.

So she continued to wait and hope.

"And the Soul Train Lady of Soul Awards for Best R&B/Soul Single goes to..."

Bey held her breath. She clutched Kelly's hand on one side and Tina's on the other. *Come on. Just say it. Please!*

"... Destiny's Child for 'No, No, No'!"

The girls – Bey, Kelly, LeToya and LaTavia – flew into a hug. Their first major award! For their very first single! They could hardly believe it.

Bey squeezed Kelly's hand tight as they stood squashed together behind the podium. Their bright dresses – made of gold, pink, green and blue sari silk – dazzled under the lights. Each girl gripped her award tightly as if it could disappear in an instant.

"LaTavia, you speak," said Bey, nodding to her.

Smiling, LaTavia gave their thank yous. Cameras flashed. The audience whooped and cheered. In the darkness, Bey could just pick out Mathew, Tina, Keith and Lonnie. She beamed towards them. What a team! Bey knew how lucky she was. So many people believed in her.

Then her mind flew to Andretta. The only person who wasn't there. *Thank you*, she thought.

You made this happen. This is your victory, too.

Once the ceremony was over, there were more photos. In fact, the cameras didn't stop flashing all night. The girls didn't stop smiling, either – they didn't want to! They posed with their awards, in the heat of the Los Angeles evening, while journalists shouted questions.

Plans for the future? A new album? The next tour?

The girls answered as briefly as possible. They didn't know what the future would hold. Who did?!

'No, No, No' sold over a million copies in the USA. Shortly after it was released, the girls set off on tour. It was their second tour. Their first had been two years ago, as support act for R&B group SWV. This time it was much, much bigger. They were supporting Boyz II Men, one of the biggest R&B bands. The tour started out in Memphis, Tennessee. The girls thought they had worked hard before, but touring took it to a whole new level!

Tennessee. Nashville. Dallas. Las Vegas. Los Angeles. San Diego. Seattle. Phoenix. Cleveland.

Chicago. Toronto. Washington DC. Atlanta. Miami... The list went on and on.

Most nights they sang at a new venue. Then, early the next morning, they set off by coach or plane to the next city. The girls travelled farther in these few months than they had in their whole lives! They stayed in fancy hotels and were driven around in limos. Each night, they ordered room service, which came on a trolley, the dishes kept warm under a silver dome. The waiters even wore white gloves, like in the movies!

But by August, the girls were exhausted. They longed for their own beds, under their own roofs. Home-cooked meals. Lazy evenings in front of the TV. Their families. Their friends...

"Come on, girls! Just three more shows. We can do this!" said Bey, smiling.

Kelly, LaTavia and LeToya were slumped on chairs in each corner of the dressing room. Clothes and accessories spilled out of suitcases on the floor. Pizza boxes were piled up on the dressing table. It was their fourth concert this week.

"My blisters are killing me," moaned Kelly. "I

can't wear these heels again. I won't be able to stand up."

"Me neither," wailed LeToya. "Remember when we used to wear sneakers instead of heels, girls?"

"Go on without me tonight," groaned LaTavia.

"We're living the dream!" Bey reminded them. "Would you seriously want to be anywhere else?"

"Yes – in bed!" the girls chorused.

"OK," agreed Bey. "We're tired. But we've only got a few more days, then it's back to Houston. Right now, you need to get your outfits on. Mom will be here to do our hair any second."

"If you want me onstage," laughed LeToya, still slumped in her seat, "you're going to have to carry me out there."

"Carry you, in these shoes? You must be kidding!"

The door opened and Tina appeared. Bey's mum did their hair for every show.

"Who's not going out tonight?" she joked.

"All of them, Mom," giggled Bey. "We have a mutiny on our hands!"

Tina smiled. The girls weren't the only ones who were tired. Bey and her friends just had to sing. Tina had to do their hair, make sure they studied, sort out their squabbles... *and* look after Solange! But it was worth it to see her girls shine onstage every night.

"So whose hair am I doing first?"

"I guess it's me, Mom," said Bey, looking round the room.

"Remind me what you're wearing tonight?"

"We're in black tonight, Miss Tina," said LaTavia, holding up a tight lace dress.

Tina frowned. These outfits weren't right. They made the girls look much too old. That and the heavy make-up. The fans of Destiny's Child were kids and teens. The outfits should be bright and memorable. It was the 90s!

Bey saw her mum's expression. She could read her mind easily. "Maybe *you* should start styling us, Mom."

"That's a thought."

Tina had plenty of ideas. Four gorgeous girls and a proper budget! If she were their stylist, they could really start having some fun...

CHAPTER 18

THE WRITING'S ON THE WALL

The final destination on the tour was Miami. After their last concert, the girls jumped into a car, determined to see the sites: Ocean Drive, the beach, the palms... Finally, the girls could have some time off!

"Enjoy it," said Mathew. "When we get back, you girls are going to be *busy*."

He wasn't joking. Now the tour had come to an end, Mathew had booked concerts, TV and radio appearances, and more recording sessions. And the most exciting news of all: Columbia Records wanted a second album from Destiny's Child!

"This time it's got to be *big*," Beyoncé told the girls.

The first album had sold a good number of copies, but Bey knew they could do better. Much better. She knew that she had *lots* more to give.

"When we were Girl's Tyme, do you remember how Tony Mo made us sit and write song lyrics?" she asked Kelly.

"Yeah, I could never think of anything to write," groaned her best friend. "I'd just stare at my notebook for ten minutes, then give up."

"I want to do that again," said Bey. "The whole group, writing. We might come up with something amazing."

"I guess." Kelly looked unsure. "Let's give it a try. We're older now. Perhaps we have more to say."

LaTavia and LeToya agreed to the plan. The record label had sent hundreds of tunes for them to listen to. Musicians and songwriters from all over the world wanted their songs to be recorded by Destiny's Child. Bey and her friends picked out the ones they liked. Then they began to write new lyrics to go with the music.

"What do you think of this?" asked Bey. She sung them her idea. The words were about falling in love. They fitted the catchy, upbeat tune she'd chosen perfectly.

"That's cool, Bey."

"Then the chorus should go afterwards."

"We need a different rhyme."

"I liked it better before. Like this..."

Often, the girls wrote about having fun or being independent. They wanted their songs to be from a female perspective, unlike many of the lyrics they received. All the girls contributed, but Beyoncé wrote the most. She didn't share her feelings often, but when it came to writing songs, her emotions seemed to come easily. Joy and upset and anger poured onto the page. The lines she wrote felt true.

Usually, Bey and her friends wrote in the recording studio. The studio manager was puzzled. Most groups had their songs ready by the time they came in to record.

"Well, we're different," said Beyoncé. "That's how *they* work. This is how *we* work."

But at last the songs were ready. Beyoncé had co-written eleven of them. They had also chosen a name for the album: *The Writing's on the Wall*.

The four girls were proud of their songs. Everyone, especially Beyoncé, had worked so hard.

But there was a problem.

The girls were used to Beyoncé singing the lead vocals. Since Ashley had left the group, Bey sang almost all the leads, occasionally sharing them with Kelly. LeToya and LaTavia sang the harmonies, giving Destiny's Child its distinctive sound.

But day after day, LeToya and LaTavia sat watching through the glass as Beyoncé sang in the recording booth. They felt left out. Why weren't they inside? Surely Bey must have finished recording her parts by now? What was going on? Was Beyoncé recording their parts as well as her own?

Eventually, the album was finished. Everyone agreed it sounded great, but LeToya and LaTavia weren't happy. As they expected, they barely featured on the recording. And they had an idea why...

"Mathew wants Bey to be the star!"

"He doesn't want anyone else to share the limelight!"

"He's not interested in us!"

Mathew tried to reassure them. Everyone in Destiny's Child was important, he told them. But LeToya and LaTavia had made up their minds: it wasn't fair and they weren't going to put up with it.

Both girls decided to leave the group.

Bey and Kelly were devastated. Suddenly, the group had shattered into pieces. They were losing their two best friends.

And that wasn't all. Since LeToya and LaTavia had left the group, the media had begun to stir up trouble. They called Beyoncé a diva. They said Mathew was a bad manager. They claimed he was only interested in Bey's success and didn't care about the other girls. Up till now, Bey had enjoyed giving interviews and being on TV. But now, no one seemed to care whether what they read about Bey and her family was true or not. It was a horrible feeling.

Back in Houston, Bey shut herself in her room for days at a time. It felt like everything she had worked for was crumbling to dust. What was the point of going on with it?

"Maybe I should go solo," said Bey. "It's too complicated being part of a group."

"We believe in you, whatever you decide," said Mathew.

But, secretly, Mathew and Tina hoped Bey would stick with Destiny's Child. There were some brilliant songs on the second album. They felt sure it would be a huge success. Fans travelled across the world to see the girls perform. It seemed too good to give up on.

But it was hard to see Bey so unhappy.

CHAPTER 19

SAY MY NAME

Shut in her room, Beyoncé tossed and turned on her bed, thinking about everything that had happened. She thought about her hopes and dreams. Bey had achieved so much. Was being in Destiny's Child what she wanted? It was just Kelly and her now. Would it be possible to continue the group with only the two of them?

Had she earned her place as the group's lead singer?

Or was it true that she got special treatment because of her dad?

Tina, Mathew and Kelly tried to comfort her. Of course she'd earned it. They loved her. Her fans loved her.

Eventually, Tina stepped in. Destiny's Child *had* to continue! They had come so far. She remembered a young woman they had met on tour. What was her name? Michelle? Michelle Williams! That was it. Tina remembered what a great singer Michelle was and had a feeling she would fit right in.

Tentatively, she suggested it to her daughter. "Bey, what if we found someone new...?"

Bey agreed. Tina was relieved – and Kelly was, too. She knew that Destiny's Child had more to give. Then Kelly remembered the name of a talented girl who had featured as an extra on one of their videos – Farrah Franklin. Perhaps they could ask her to audition as well...

Michelle and Farrah hurried to Houston. They were excited about the idea of auditioning for Destiny's Child. Both girls impressed both Mathew and Bey. They had great voices and plenty of personality.

"Would you like the job?" Mathew asked them.

How could they say no?!

Bey and Kelly hugged the new girls with delight. Destiny's Child had four brilliant singers again. Phew! Beyoncé smiled with relief. Things were going to be all right.

Although the girls missed LeToya and LaTavia, it was fun to get to know Michelle and Farrah. They liked the new girls immediately.

And the fans did, too.

Just a few weeks ago, Michelle and Farrah had been unknown. Now they were playing concerts, travelling by limo, flying first class and staying in luxury hotels. They were doing interviews on TV and radio. Everywhere they went, there were cheering crowds and flashing cameras. It had been a crazy few weeks for everyone.

Destiny's Child had recorded their second album, *The Writing's on the Wall*, before LeToya and LaTavia left the group. They were proud of all the songs on it. Bey was particularly excited about 'Say My Name'. All four girls had helped to write it. The song would be released as a single in a few months' time, and Bey had a feeling it was special.

She was right. 'Say My Name' was Destiny's Child's biggest hit so far.

"Three weeks at the top of the pop *and* R&B charts," said Mathew proudly. "I think you've made it, girls!"

Those were big words – but as the weeks went on, it looked like they might be true. 'Say My Name' won the group their first Grammy. *The Writing's on the Wall* stayed in the charts for an incredible 99 consecutive weeks. It was the girls' second platinum album, selling over eight million copies in the US alone.

They really had made it – and all of them knew there was so much more to come!

In spring 2000, Destiny's Child flew to Cancún, Mexico, to perform at MTV's Spring Break. By now, Michelle and Farrah were used to the hectic DC schedule. Being on the plane was a chance to rest and chat and catch up on beauty sleep. And, no matter how famous they had become, it was still fun to stare around first class and point out the celebs to one another.

But when they arrived in Cancún... Disaster.

Tina and her assistant had been waiting at

the baggage carousel for half an hour. The rest of the passengers from their flight had come and gone. Luggage from another flight had begun to tumble down onto the carousel. Where were their suitcases?

Bey and the girls were waiting in the first-class lounge – hidden behind their dark glasses from any lurking paparazzi – when Tina came rushing in.

"Girls, our luggage is lost! It wasn't on the plane," she wailed.

"Our costumes..." cried Bey.

"We need to be onstage in a few hours!" Kelly shrieked. "What are we going to do?"

The girls began to panic.

"Maybe we could wear what we're wearing now?" Bey was dressed down in jeans, a T-shirt and a sparkly baseball cap. She shrugged. It wasn't great, but...

"No! No way!" Tina sounded horrified. She had spent weeks planning and sewing outfits for the four girls. She thought sadly about her glamorous designs, the bright, beautiful fabrics, a different style for each girl...

"Why can't we buy costumes here?" asked Michelle. "There must be stores."

"The fans," said Beyoncé quickly. "We can't."

The other girls instantly knew what she meant. They were famous now! Everywhere they went, they were followed by fans and the paparazzi. There was only one option.

"Leave it to me," said Tina. "Give me an hour and I'll sort it out."

"Thanks, Mom. Good luck!"

Tina jumped into a taxi while Bey, Kelly, Michelle and Farrah climbed into their waiting limo. They hoped Tina would find what she was looking for, or their fans would be very disappointed. Their fans expected style. They expected flair. They expected Destiny's Child!

Tina arrived at the hotel less than an hour later. She burst into Bey's room, beaming from ear to ear. But she wasn't carrying shopping bags. Instead, her arms were full of fabric: a stiff material, the pattern made up of splodges of grey and black on a khaki background.

Camouflage?!

Tina sank into a chair and the camouflage fabric spilled onto the floor.

"What are you doing, Mom? We're singers, not soldiers! We can't wear this!"

"I bought it at the local market." Tina smiled. "Trust me. You're going to look great. Better than ever!"

Wow. This was different. But Bey trusted her mum and she liked the idea of surprising her audience.

"Go and hang out with the other girls," her mum told her. "I need space. I haven't got much time."

"Yes, Mom!"

That was the trouble with bringing your mum on tour. Sometimes even a famous singer couldn't help feeling like a little child again!

After only an hour, Tina called the girls back in. She handed them each an outfit – trousers for Kelly and Michelle, shorts for Farrah and a dress for Beyoncé. All were made from the camouflage fabric.

"These are incredible!" cried Kelly.

"Wow! I love it!" gushed Michelle.

"They're so *us*," squealed Farrah.

Bey felt proud of her mum. When there was a problem, Tina always knew what to do.

"You're our fairy godmother, Mom," she said.

"I don't remember Cinderella wearing khaki," laughed Tina.

"Didn't your mother make clothes too, Tina?" asked Kelly.

"My mom was a dressmaker. If she had been alive today, I think she would have been famous. She had an amazing imagination."

"Like you, Mom." Bey smiled.

Wearing the new outfits, their hair quickly styled, the girls jumped into their limo. They had just enough time to get to the seafront before the start of the show. The stage had been set on the beach, fringed by palm trees. Led by Beyoncé, the girls ran onstage, clapping their hands above their heads, their hair whipped by the sea breeze.

"Love the look!" shouted one fan.

"Khaki rocks!" hollered another. "We love you, Destiny's Child!"

The girls felt amazing. In front of them was a sea of screaming fans. Behind them was the sparkling turquoise ocean. Tina's impromptu costumes, made with love, were perfect for this beautiful location. Bey had sung hundreds of concerts, but she knew she would remember Cancún and this stunning seafront show for the rest of her life.

"So, you lost your luggage?"

The plane carrying Bey and the girls was cruising at maximum altitude, bound for home. Bey was still bubbling with excitement from yesterday's outdoor performance. Offstage she could still be shy, especially with strangers. Not today, though. The young man in the seat next to her listened, smiling, as she told the story of the costume emergency.

"My mom made outfits out of camouflage fabric. It was crazy."

The man laughed. "I saw your show."

"And?"

"You were seriously good."

Bey smiled. Everyone told her how good she was: her parents, her sister, her friends, her fans.

It was weird, though – she had never been happier to hear it than today, from the man in the seat next to her.

"I'm Beyoncé," she told him.

"I know," he grinned. "I'm Jay Z."

Bey smiled. "I know!"

CHAPTER 20

SURVIVOR

It was July and Destiny's Child was about to go on tour again. Their destination was Australia, almost ten thousand miles away. It would take the girls over twenty hours to get there.

"Where's Farrah?" asked Bey, nervously watching the departures board in the first-class lounge. "She's going to miss the flight if she's not here soon."

Michelle and Kelly stared anxiously at Bey as she paced back and forth across the room. Something wasn't right. Why wasn't Farrah here? Why hadn't she rung?

Suddenly, Bey's ringtone sounded. She answered. The girls watched her frown then shake her head.

"You can't," she said. "No, you can't!"

Michelle and Kelly looked at each other. What was going on?

"If you don't get here now," Bey continued, "you're out of Destiny's Child."

There was silence. Kelly and Michelle couldn't hear what Farrah was saying on the other end of the line. Bey had looked angry, but now she turned pale.

"I see. OK. Goodbye."

Bey slumped into a seat and put her head in her hands. "I'm sorry, girls. Farrah's not coming. She's out, and she's not coming back."

Kelly and Michelle stared at Beyoncé in horror. Things hadn't felt right with Farrah for a while. But now she was gone! Just like that! Could they still go on tour? Just the three of them?

Bey read their minds. "We're going to Australia without her. We don't need Farrah Franklin."

And it turned out they didn't. A few days later, when the three girls stepped onstage as a trio, it felt like a new beginning. This was it. This was Destiny's Child: Beyoncé, Kelly, Michelle.

But for the media, it was another opportunity

to attack Bey and her family. Just as when LeToya and LaTavia left the group, the journalists pounced. Why had Farrah left? They simply wouldn't let the question go.

Bey's mind flew back to school. It was like being bullied, but this time she couldn't go home to escape. There was nowhere to hide. The bullies were everywhere – on the TV, on the Internet, in the papers, on the front covers of magazines...

Just today, a DJ had made fun of the group. Live on the radio! To thousands of listeners!

"You know the show Survivor? That's what Destiny's Child is like! Who will be voted off next...?"

Survivor was a reality TV show where contestants voted each other off an island. But it wasn't Bey who had voted LeToya, LaTavia and Farrah out of Destiny's Child!

Alone in her hotel room, Beyoncé fumed.

And, suddenly, an idea popped into her head. Bey reached for a pen and notepad, and she began to scribble. With every line she wrote, she knew she was turning a bad situation into something good.

Something magical was happening.

Bey called her new song 'Survivor'. She grinned every time she thought about that radio DJ. What would he say when he realised she had turned his hurtful words into a powerful anthem?

Beyoncé didn't know it, but she had written Destiny's Child's greatest hit yet. For now, it was enough to feel happy again. She had taken control; the media couldn't hurt her. As the weeks went by, she was writing more and more songs. She had started to produce some of them, too. As a young artist, she had always asked so many questions. Now, sitting in the recording studio, she knew the sounds she wanted and how to create them. She felt as good here as she did onstage.

Following 'Survivor', the hits came thick and fast:

'Jumpin', Jumpin'.
'Bills, Bills, Bills'.
'Bug a Boo'.

Then the girls recorded 'Independent Woman'. It was simple and punchy. The lyrics showed how women could earn their own success; they could make money; they didn't need to depend on men. Mathew decided to send it to the film studio remaking *Charlie's Angels*. The director loved it! The message celebrating powerful women and girls was perfect. He wanted to make it the film's signature song.

Their first movie theme song!

The track spent an astonishing eleven weeks at number one. Destiny's Child wasn't just surviving, it was flying higher than ever!

"I'm going to be in a movie, Kelly," announced Bey.

Bey and Kelly were back at home in Houston. It was rare for them to have a few days off. It was good to spend some family time together– and enjoy a bit of home cooking.

A movie! That wasn't what Kelly had expected to hear. Months earlier – while recording 'Survivor' – Bey, Kelly and Michelle had agreed to take a break from Destiny's Child to make some solo music. All three girls had big plans. But this was... wow!

"I don't know if I can act," said Bey. "But I want to try."

Kelly nodded. Her friend was always eager to try new things, to push herself. She thought of the video diaries they had made for MTV. Bey was a natural in front of the camera.

"You'll be amazing, honestly!"

"There's singing, too; it's called *Carmen: A Hip Hopera.*"

Carmen? It was the story of a beautiful, passionate young woman who is determined not to be controlled by the men around her. Kelly smiled. That sounded just right for her friend Bey!

Beyoncé loved being on the film set, learning a new way of performing. The director coached her to deliver her lines with power and emotion. Bey was good at writing about her feelings, and now she was learning to let them show onscreen. Not everything came easily, though. Bey had never kissed anyone in front of the camera. She was so nervous! The other actors couldn't help laughing. Beyoncé the singer, how could she be scared of a screen kiss?

But Bey soon overcame her fears. Like everything else, she practised. If she could do this, she told herself, she could do anything.

In addition to her fellow actors, Bey also enjoyed meeting the people who worked behind the scenes. She had always valued the skills and hard work of her crew. It was great to feel part of one big family, working together day after day to create something.

And *Carmen* was about to lead to something much, much bigger...

Mike Myers wanted Beyoncé to star in his third *Austin Powers* film. The part? Foxxy Cleopatra, a singer and undercover spy – and Austin's girlfriend. The film had a vast budget. It was packed with star names.

Bey was nervous. Could she do it? The film was a comedy. In Destiny's Child, it was Michelle who was the joker. Bey was the sensible one, the serious one.

But Bey was always up for a challenge. Maybe it was time to get in touch with her silly side. Mike Myers and his team certainly seemed to think she could do it!

While Beyoncé was back on set, acting in her first major movie, Michelle and Kelly were busy working on solo albums. The fans of Destiny's Child were waiting eagerly. Michelle's album was released first. Then Kelly's. Would there be a solo album from Beyoncé, too?

In every spare moment she had, Bey was writing songs. Once her film was finished, she planned to go straight back to the recording studio.

Austin Powers in Goldmember was released in 2002. The movie was a huge hit. It featured a new song by Beyoncé: 'Work it Out'. Bey's acting surprised everyone, too. She was engaging, controlled – and funny!

Seriously... was there anything Beyoncé Knowles couldn't do?!

CHAPTER 21

CRAZY IN LOVE

Onscreen, Beyoncé had found love as Austin Powers' girlfriend, Foxxy Cleopatra. But what about in real life? Bey was no longer dating Lyndall Locke. Her busy touring schedule, travelling round America and the world, had made it impossible. There *was* someone Bey had been getting close to, though...

The man in the seat next to hers on that plane back from Cancún.

A rapper and global megastar.

Jay Z.

For more than a year, Bey and Jay had been speaking on the phone, getting to know one another. Bey had sung on one of his records. Now, Bey wanted

Jay to return the favour and rap on her new song, 'Crazy in Love'.

Jay agreed at once. A few weeks later, he went into the studio with her and improvised his rap section. It took only a few minutes.

"You inspired me," he told her. "It's a great song."

Bey nodded. This song had come together like magic. She believed in it.

All the same, she knew she must be cautious. Her first solo single had come out a few months earlier. The response had been disappointing. Bey had struggled to get the support of her record label to release an album. "None of these songs are hits," they had told her. Beyoncé had won the argument; the album was going ahead. But she knew it needed to be big, or her solo career would be over before it had begun.

The songs were recorded. It had taken many months, working with songwriters and artists from all over the world. All she could do now was wait.

Meanwhile, everyone – Kelly, Michelle, Mathew, Tina, Solange – had the same question. Was Bey in love with Jay Z?

Of course, Bey wouldn't tell them! Her love life was private. It always had been.

But keeping a secret of any kind was about to get much harder...

It was 23rd June 2003. The time had finally come. Beyoncé's first solo album, *Dangerously in Love*, was out today. Bey held her breath. What would her fans think? What would the critics say? Who would be proved right – Beyoncé or her record label?

The response was incredible! 'Crazy in Love' was the song of the summer. It shot to number one in America and across Europe. It was playing on every radio, at every party, in every mall and every store. Beyoncé's name was on everyone's lips.

And it wasn't only 'Crazy in Love' that reached number one. Bey had four more number-one hits that year. She had wanted to make songs to dance to and songs to cry to; a mix of R&B, hip-hop, soul and reggae. It turned out her fans wanted the same thing.

Dangerously in Love sold over twelve million copies worldwide. Twelve million! Beyoncé won five more Grammy Awards. Only three other female artists had won as many awards in one night.

"I'm so proud of you," Jay told her.

Bey had never been happier. She and Jay were together at last – officially. Kelly and Michelle had launched successful solo albums. And now Bey was a bestselling solo artist, too!

It felt to Bey like there were fireworks going off all around her. No, it felt like *she* was the firework – sparkling, shimmering, rocketing through the atmosphere, higher and higher, as the world watched in awe!

But the real challenge lay ahead. Up till now, Bey had promoted her music with Kelly and Michelle. How would she manage on her own? Her first solo tour. Her first solo interviews. Magazine covers. TV commercials, even.

Sometimes it was lonely, but Bey kept her focus. She seized every opportunity that a solo career offered. The highlight? Bey was invited to sing the National Anthem at the 2004 Super Bowl in Houston. It was her childhood dream! Famous as she was, Bey felt just like a small kid who had been picked to sing in a school concert. Except this time it would be in front of millions.

For a year, Bey worked tirelessly. Her family could see how much she missed Kelly and Michelle, though. One day, Mathew made a suggestion: was it time for Destiny's Child to come back together, for one last album and tour? All three girls had proved themselves as solo performers. He knew their fans would love to see them reunited!

Bey agreed at once. So did Kelly and Michelle.

So the girls went straight back to the studio to record *Destiny Fulfilled*, their fourth album. They were so happy to be together again, especially when the tour began. It felt amazing to stand backstage before a performance and stack their hands one on top of another like they used to do. And their fans were overjoyed to see them sing as Destiny's Child one final time.

The tour ended all too quickly. But each of the girls had exciting plans. It was time to move on. Kelly was returning to the studio to record more music. Michelle was, too.

"What are you going to do next, Bey?" asked Kelly.

Bey smiled. Her wish list grew longer every day.

"First, another film," she told her. "I've been offered the lead role in *Dreamgirls*."

Dreamgirls was based on the story of Diana Ross and The Supremes. The girls knew that Diana was one of Bey's greatest heroes.

"And then?"

"I'm going to buy a house."

Actually, Bey planned to buy several. Her parents had split up for good now – but they were still close. She dreamed of buying two neighbouring apartments in New York, one for each of them.

"What about music?" asked Kelly.

"I've got ideas." Bey grinned. This was a secret she wouldn't share, even with her closest friend.

"And Jay?" Kelly already knew what the answer to this would be – and she was right.

"Wait and see!" laughed Bey.

CHAPTER 22

HISTORY IN THE MAKING

In fact, it was less than a year before Bey, Kelly and Michelle were reunited again. The place? Los Angeles. The occasion? To unveil a star for Destiny's Child on the Hollywood Walk of Fame!

"Dreams come true. Thank you all so much for supporting us," Bey told the crowds who had gathered to watch.

Ever since they had first walked along Hollywood Boulevard, Bey, Kelly and Michelle had dreamed about a star of their own. Now, here it was, in glittering marble and bronze!

By now, Bey's second solo album, *B'Day*, was out and she was planning her next tour, The Beyoncé

Experience. She had an aim: to create a concert experience no one would ever forget. She wanted her show to be *epic*. More props! More costume changes! More dancers! More musicians!

Thousands of women had auditioned to be in Bey's new all-female band, Suga Mama. Bey wanted to encourage all girls to play instruments. It wasn't only boys who could be in bands! She was passionate about helping a new generation of girls to grow up and follow their dreams.

When the tour finally hit the road, it was a triumph. Fans and critics agreed: Beyoncé was one of the greatest live performers *ever*. Finally, she had created a show worthy of her hero, Michael Jackson.

But there was still one thing missing. Bey hadn't had a big hit since 'Crazy in Love'. She needed another massive song. Something iconic. A game-changer.

Finally – finally! – Bey knew she had found it.

'Crazy in Love' had been big – but 'Single Ladies (Put a Ring on It)' was *enormous*.

This time, it wasn't just DJs playing it and fans singing it. People on the street were using Bey's lyrics in everyday conversations. The video – Bey and two other dancers, shot in black-and-white – launched hundreds of memes. Bey couldn't believe it. This was the simplest video she had ever made – the cheapest, too!

Her song had become a cultural phenomenon.

'Single Ladies' also won six Grammys, the most awards ever won by a female artist in one night.

Queen Bey was on her way to becoming one of the biggest artists in the world.

So, had she ticked everything off her wish list now?

Well, not quite...

On 4 April 2008, Bey and Jay got married in Jay's penthouse apartment in New York. The ceremony took place in a huge marquee on the roof, decorated with seventy thousand perfect white orchids, Bey's favourite flower. By now, Bey's friends and family were used to luxury and glamour, but this was something else!

For Bey, Jay and their families, it was one of the most magical days of their lives.

It was true that Bey and Jay lived a life of luxury. They owned several mansions and apartments, and moved secretly between them in helicopters and limos, like spies. But both megastars knew how important it was to share their success. Bey used her profile to support many charities. She had become a passionate spokesperson for important causes: homelessness, unemployment, food poverty, gender and racial equality, and disaster relief. She set up The Survivor Foundation with Kelly, to help victims of Hurricane Katrina. A few years later, she would also set up the BeyGood Foundation, raising money for charities all over the world. She and Jay both gave millions of dollars to charity.

Her good work, like her talent, did not go unnoticed.

In 2009, Barack Obama became President of the USA. He asked Bey to sing at his inauguration ball. It was a momentous invitation. How could she refuse! America had elected its first black president – this was history in the making. Beyoncé had supported Obama's election campaign throughout. She believed in his message of opportunity for all.

Her heart swelled with pride as she sang in front of Barack and Michelle Obama, world leaders and A-list celebrities. How amazing it was to be part of this moment!

Bey didn't know it yet, but she would perform again at Obama's second inauguration, singing the National Anthem, 'The Star-Spangled Banner'. This time she would sing in front of an entire nation, watching on TV.

If Beyoncé's life was a song, the beat was getting faster and faster, the music louder and louder!

By now, Bey had sung on every continent except Antarctica. Her fans numbered hundreds of millions. They even gave themselves a name: the Beyhive.

Queen Bey was the bestselling female artist of the decade, winner of twenty Grammys, nominated for more awards than any other woman in music history.

And she had just become a mother.

Blue Ivy Carter was born in New York in 2012. The name 'Ivy' was a sort of code: IV meant 4 in roman numerals. Four was a special number for Bey and Jay. When she got older, their little daughter would come to know how special she was, too.

Sitting beside Bey's hospital bed in New York, Tina cradled her newborn granddaughter and smiled to herself. She remembered the conversation she'd had with her father, Lumis, when Beyoncé was born. How important a name was! She knew she had chosen well – and so had her daughter.

Mathew was also delighted to be a grandparent. The last few months had been hard for him. Although Mathew still managed Solange, herself now a successful singer, Beyoncé had decided to set up her own management company.

"I couldn't have done this without you, Dad," she told him. "You did an incredible job. But I'm grown-up now. I need to make my own decisions."

Bey also wanted to do things differently. She knew her audience liked to be surprised... so she released her fifth album, *Beyoncé*, in secret. Her fans knew nothing about the album until it appeared, like magic, online. Even the dancers appearing in the video didn't know which artist they were working for!

Bey's next surprise was bigger still: twin babies, a girl and a boy, named Rumi and Sir. Bey never shared much of her private life online, but a few carefully chosen photos of the twins set the Beyhive buzzing for months!

Meanwhile, Bey's shows were getting more and more spectacular. It took seven Boeing 747s and 70 lorries to move her *Formation* tour from one country to the next. She sang for more than two hours, performing more than thirty songs, with seven costume changes. Giant screens projected videos and positive messages to inspire young girls, people of colour, men and women from every background...

Across the world, hundreds of millions of fans waited to see what Beyoncé would do next. They knew it would be big. They knew it would be different. Bey never stood still.

Best of all, though, they loved Bey's message: follow your dreams. When Beyoncé told her fans that they could do anything, be anything, they believed it.

Why wouldn't they? Queen Bey was the proof!

Turn the page for a sneak preview of another inspiring *Ultimate Superstars* story...

ARIANA GRANDE

Available now!

978-178-7-414-778

CHAPTER 1

ONE LOVE

The sun was shining when Ariana entered the stage at Old Trafford in Manchester on Sunday 4, June, 2017. Dressed in a simple white sweatshirt with 'One Love: Manchester' printed across the front, ripped blue jeans and killer-heeled boots, Ariana dazzled as always. But there was something else behind her wide smile and sparkling eyes. There was sadness, determination, but, above all, love. As soon as the crowd saw her, there was a surge of excitement – love really did fill the air!

Take That, Robbie Williams, Pharrell Williams and Miley Cyrus had already done their thing at the One Love concert. Robbie Williams was in bits as he sang 'Angels' – at times, the crowd had to sing the words for him, just to get through the song. Then Pharrell and Miley had raised the mood with 'Get Lucky' and 'Happy'. But it was Ariana the crowd were here to see, and when she opened with 'Be Alright', they were joyful. She was back: singing, dancing, smiling and swinging that ponytail, like only Ariana could.

Later, she teamed up with Victoria Monet, The Black Eyed Peas, Miley Cyrus, Coldplay and even a local school choir. Throughout the concert, Ariana's love and admiration for the people of Manchester shone brightly.

For 'One Last Time', the whole cast of One Love Manchester joined Ariana onstage. Ariana looked around at the famous artists gathered at her side – how had it come to this? She did her best to push the memories of the tragedy just a few weeks ago from her mind. If she thought about that devastating night too much, she knew she'd break down and cry – and never stop! She hugged Katy Perry and Miley Cyrus. Somehow that helped to keep the tears from falling.

And all too soon, it was the final song of the

evening. Ariana walked to the front of the stage. The sky had darkened to midnight blue, but the lights from the rig shone brightly on her face.

"Thank you so much. I love you," she told the cheering crowd for the zillionth time that night – and she meant it. And then she closed her eyes and pulled the microphone in close, as the opening notes to 'Somewhere Over the Rainbow' played. Ariana began to sing. As ever, her voice took effortless flight as she belted out the well-loved song.

Wow! If only the audience knew how much this song meant to Ariana. Back when she was a little girl, she used to sing it with her grandfather. 'Grande' was her favourite person in the world, but he'd died a few years ago. He'd always told her to sing 'Somewhere Over the Rainbow' at the end of a concert. It hadn't happened yet... but this last week, there was a voice inside Ariana that told her this was the perfect song to close the concert tonight. And now that she was actually here onstage in Manchester, singing it, she could sense the spirit of her grandfather, right there beside her. She felt a lump in her throat...

When Ariana opened her eyes, she could see the crowd swaying, and twinkling lights and flags waving gently in the night air. The audience were starstruck and many of them were in tears. *Boy, it's hard to sing when you're about to cry*, she thought to herself as she stumbled over a few words. *But this is what love looks like*, Ariana realised, as her own eyes began to fill up.

It had been Ariana's idea to stage this emotional event. The bomb attack at her concert, in this city less than two weeks before, had shaken the world. Getting up and singing was the only way she felt she could help the victims of this terrible tragedy. The money they raised would help the families who had lost so much. And, by getting up and performing again, Ariana wanted to prove that love does conquer hate. That night, Ariana delivered her heartfelt message of love, and people applauded her for her courage and dignity.